ALSO BY PAUL MULDOON

SELECTED POEMS

1968–2014

SELECTED POEMS
1968–2014

PAUL MULDOON

FARRAR, STRAUS AND GIROUX

NEW YORK

Farrar, Straus and Giroux
18 West 18th Street, New York 10011

Printed in the United States of America
Originally published in 2016 by Faber & Faber Limited, Great Britain
Published in the United States in 2016 by Farrar, Straus and Giroux
First American paperback edition, 2017

The Library of Congress has cataloged the hardcover edition as follows:
Names: Muldoon, Paul, author.
Title: Selected poems 1968–2014 / Paul Muldoon.
Description: First American edition. | New York : Farrar, Straus
    and Giroux, 2016. | Includes index.
Identifiers: LCCN 2016033242 | ISBN 9780374260828 (hardback) |
    ISBN 9780374715779 (e-book)
Subjects: BISAC: POETRY / English, Irish, Scottish, Welsh.
Classification: LCC PR6063.U367 A6 2016b | DDC 821/.914—dc23
LC record available at https://lccn.loc.gov/2016033242

Paperback ISBN: 978-0-374-53730-2

Our books may be purchased in bulk for promotional,
educational, or business use. Please contact your local bookseller
or the Macmillan Corporate and Premium Sales Department at
1-800-221-7945, extension 5442, or by e-mail at
MacmillanSpecialMarkets@macmillan.com.

www.fsgbooks.com
www.twitter.com/fsgbooks • www.facebook.com/fsgbooks

1   3   5   7   9   10   8   6   4   2

Contents

SELECTED POEMS

1968–2014

from NEW WEATHER

Wind and Tree

In the way that the most of the wind
Happens where there are trees,

Most of the world is centred
About ourselves.

Often where the wind has gathered
The trees together and together,

One tree will take
Another in her arms and hold.

Their branches that are grinding
Madly together and together,

It is no real fire.
They are breaking each other.

Often I think I should be like
The single tree, going nowhere,

Since my own arm could not and would not
Break the other. Yet by my broken bones

I tell new weather.

Dancers at the Moy

This Italian square
And circling plain
Black once with mares
And their stallions,
The flat Blackwater
Turning its stones

Over hour after hour
As their hooves shone
And lifted together
Under the black rain,
One or other Greek war
Now coloured the town

Blacker than ever before
With hungry stallions
And their hungry mares
Like hammocks of skin,
The flat Blackwater
Unable to contain

Itself as horses poured
Over acres of grain
In a black and gold river.
No band of Athenians
Arrived at the Moy fair
To buy for their campaign,

Peace having been declared
And a treaty signed.
The black and gold river
Ended as a trickle of brown
Where those horses tore
At briars and whins,

Ate the flesh of each other
Like people in famine.
The flat Blackwater
Hobbled on its stones
With a wild stagger
And sag in its backbone,

The local people gathered
Up the white skeletons.
Horses buried for years
Under the foundations
Give their earthen floors
The ease of trampolines.

Good Friday, 1971. Driving Westward

It was good going along with the sun
Through Ballygawley, Omagh and Strabane.
I started out as it was getting light
And caught sight of hares all along the road
That looked to have been taking a last fling,
Doves making the most of their offerings
As if all might not be right with the day

Where I moved through morning towards the sea.
I was glad that I would not be alone.
Those children who travel badly as wine
Waved as they passed in their uppity cars
And now the first cows were leaving the byres,
The first lorry had delivered its load.
A whole country was fresh after the night

Though people were still fighting for the last
Dreams and changing their faces where I paused
To read the first edition of the truth.
I gave a lift to the girl out of love
And crossed the last great frontier at Lifford.
Marooned by an iffing and butting herd
Of sheep, Letterkenny had just then laid

Open its heart and we passed as new blood
Back into the grey flesh of Donegal.
The sky went out of its way for the hills
And life was changing down for the sharp bends
Where the road had put its thin brown arm round
A hill and held on tight out of pure fear.
Errigal stepped out suddenly in our

Path and the thin arm tightened round the waist
Of the mountain and for a time I lost
Control and she thought we hit something big
But I had seen nothing, perhaps a stick
Lying across the road. I glanced back once
And there was nothing but a heap of stones.
We had just dropped in from nowhere for lunch

In Gaoth Dobhair, I happy and she convinced
Of the death of more than lamb or herring.
She stood up there and then, face full of drink,
And announced that she and I were to blame
For something killed along the way we came.
Children were warned that it was rude to stare,
Left with their parents for a breath of air.

Hedgehog

The snail moves like a
Hovercraft, held up by a
Rubber cushion of itself,
Sharing its secret

With the hedgehog. The hedgehog
Shares its secret with no one.
We say, Hedgehog, come out
Of yourself and we will love you.

We mean no harm. We want
Only to listen to what
You have to say. We want
Your answers to our questions.

The hedgehog gives nothing
Away, keeping itself to itself.
We wonder what a hedgehog
Has to hide, why it so distrusts.

We forget the god
Under this crown of thorns.
We forget that never again
Will a god trust in the world.

The Year of the Sloes, for Ishi

In the Moon
Of Frost in the Tepees,
There were two stars
That got free.
They yawned and stretched
To white hides,
One cutting a slit
In the wall of itself
And stepping out into the night.

In the Moon
Of the Dark Red Calf,
It had learned
To track itself
By following the dots
And dashes of its blood.
It knew the silence
Deeper
Than that of birds not singing.

In the Moon
Of the Snowblind,
The other fed the fire
At its heart
With the dream of a deer
Over its shoulder.
One water would wade through another,
Shivering,
Salmon of Knowledge leap the Fall.

In the Moon
Of the Red Grass Appearing,
He discovered her
Lying under a bush.
There were patches of yellowed
Snow and ice
Where the sun had not looked.
He helped her over the Black Hills
To the Ford of the Two Friends.

In the Moon
Of the Ponies Shedding,
He practised counting coups,
Knowing it harder
To live at the edge of the earth
Than its centre.
He caught the nondescript horse
And stepped
Down onto the prairies.

In the Moon
Of Making the Fat,
He killed his first bison.
Her quick knife ran under the skin
And offered the heart
To the sky.
They had been the horizon.
She saved what they could not eat
That first evening.

In the Moon
Of the Red Cherries,
She pledged that she would stay
So long as there would be
The Two-Legged
And the Four-Legged Ones,
Long as grass would grow and water
Flow, and the wind blow.
None of these things had forgotten.

In the Moon
Of the Black Cherries,
While he was looking for a place
To winter,
He discovered two wagons
Lying side by side
That tried to be a ring.
There were others in blue shirts
Felling trees for a square.

In the Moon
When the Calf Grows Hair,
There was a speck in the sky
Where he had left the tepee.
An eagle had started
Out of her side
And was waiting to return.
The fire was not cold,
The feet of six horses not circles.

In the Moon
Of the Season Changing,
He left the river
Swollen with rain.
He kicked sand over the fire.
He prepared his breast
By an ochre
That none would see his blood.
Any day now would be good to die.

In the Moon
Of the Leaves Falling,
I had just taken a bite out of the
Moon and pushed the plate
Of the world away.
Someone was asking for six troopers
Who had lain down
One after another
To drink a shrieking river.

In the Moon
Of the Trees Popping, two snails
Glittered over a dead Indian.
I realized that if his brothers
Could be persuaded to lie still,
One beside the other
Right across the Great Plains,
Then perhaps something of this original
Beauty would be retained.

14

from MULES

Ned Skinner

Was 'a barbaric yawp',
If you took Aunt Sarah at her word.
He would step over the mountain
Of a summer afternoon
To dress a litter of pigs
On my uncle's farm.

Aunt Sarah would keep me in,
Taking me on her lap
Till it was over.
Ned Skinner wiped his knife
And rinsed his hands
In the barrel at the door-step.

He winked, and gripped my arm.
'It doesn't hurt, not so's you'd notice,
And God never slams one door
But another's lying open.
Them same pigs can see the wind.'
My uncle had given him five shillings.

Ned Skinner came back
While my uncle was in the fields.
'Sarah,' he was calling, 'Sarah.
You weren't so shy in our young day.
You remember yon time in Archer's loft?'
His face blazed at the scullery window.
'Remember? When the hay was won.'

Aunt Sarah had the door on the snib.
'That's no kind of talk
To be coming over. Now go you home.'
Silence. Then a wheeze.
We heard the whiskey-jug
Tinkle, his boots diminish in the yard.
Aunt Sarah put on a fresh apron.

Ma

Old photographs would have her bookish, sitting
Under a willow. I take that to be a croquet
Lawn. She reads aloud, no doubt from Rupert Brooke.
The month is always May or June.

Or with the stranger on the motor-bike.
Not my father, no. This one's all crew-cut
And polished brass buttons.
An American soldier, perhaps.
                                        And the full moon
Swaying over Keenaghan, the orchards and the cannery,
Thins to a last yellow-hammer, and goes.
The neighbours gather, all Keenaghan and Collegelands,
There is story-telling. Old miners at Coalisland
Going into the ground. Swinging, for fear of the gas,
The soft flame of a canary.

The Mixed Marriage

My father was a servant-boy.
When he left school at eight or nine
He took up billhook and loy
To win the ground he would never own.

My mother was the school-mistress,
The world of Castor and Pollux.
There were twins in her own class.
She could never tell which was which.

She had read one volume of Proust,
He knew the cure for farcy.
I flitted between a hole in the hedge
And a room in the Latin Quarter.

When she had cleared the supper-table
She opened *The Acts of the Apostles*,
Aesop's Fables, *Gulliver's Travels*.
Then my mother went on upstairs

And my father further dimmed the light
To get back to hunting with ferrets
Or the factions of the faction-fights,
The Ribbon Boys, the Caravats.

Duffy's Circus

Once Duffy's Circus had shaken out its tent
In the big field near the Moy
God may as well have left Ireland
And gone up a tree. My father had said so.

There was no such thing as the five-legged calf,
The God of Creation
Was the God of Love.
My father chose to share such Nuts of Wisdom.

Yet across the Alps of each other the elephants
Trooped. Nor did it matter
When Wild Bill's Rain Dance
Fell flat. Some clown emptied a bucket of stars

Over the swankiest part of the crowd.
I had lost my father in the rush and slipped
Out the back. Now I heard
For the first time that long-drawn-out cry.

It came from somewhere beyond the corral.
A dwarf on stilts. Another dwarf.
I sidled past some trucks. From under a freighter
I watched a man sawing a woman in half.

Mules

Should they not have the best of both worlds?

Her feet of clay gave the lie
To the star burned in our mare's brow.
Would Parsons' jackass not rest more assured
That cross wrenched from his shoulders?

We had loosed them into one field.
I watched Sam Parsons and my quick father
Tense for the punch below their belts,
For what was neither one thing or the other.

It was as though they had shuddered
To think, of their gaunt, sexless foal
Dropped tonight in the cowshed.

We might yet claim that it sprang from earth
Were it not for the afterbirth
Trailed like some fine, silk parachute,
That we would know from what heights it fell.

from WHY BROWNLEE LEFT

The Weepies

Most Saturday afternoons
At the local Hippodrome
Saw the Pathé News rooster,
Then the recurring dream

Of a lonesome drifter
Through uninterrupted range.
Will Hunter, so gifted
He could peel an orange

In a single, fluent gesture,
Was the leader of our gang.
The curtain rose this afternoon
On a lion, not a gong.

When the crippled girl
Who wanted to be a dancer
Met the married man
Who was dying of cancer,

Our hankies unfurled
Like flags of surrender.
I believe something fell asunder
In even Will Hunter's hands.

Cuba

My eldest sister arrived home that morning
In her white muslin evening dress.
'Who the hell do you think you are,
Running out to dances in next to nothing?
As though we hadn't enough bother
With the world at war, if not at an end.'
My father was pounding the breakfast-table.

'Those Yankees were touch and go as it was –
If you'd heard Patton in Armagh –
But this Kennedy's nearly an Irishman
So he's not much better than ourselves.
And him with only to say the word.
If you've got anything on your mind
Maybe you should make your peace with God.'

I could hear May from beyond the curtain.
'Bless me, Father, for I have sinned.
I told a lie once, I was disobedient once.
And, Father, a boy touched me once.'
'Tell me, child. Was this touch immodest?
Did he touch your breast, for example?'
'He brushed against me, Father. Very gently.'

Anseo

When the Master was calling the roll
At the primary school in Collegelands,
You were meant to call back *Anseo*
And raise your hand
As your name occurred.
Anseo, meaning here, here and now,
All present and correct,
Was the first word of Irish I spoke.
The last name on the ledger
Belonged to Joseph Mary Plunkett Ward
And was followed, as often as not,
By silence, knowing looks,
A nod and a wink, the Master's droll
'And where's our little Ward-of-court?'

I remember the first time he came back
The Master had sent him out
Along the hedges
To weigh up for himself and cut
A stick with which he would be beaten.
After a while, nothing was spoken;
He would arrive as a matter of course
With an ash-plant, a salley-rod.
Or, finally, the hazel-wand
He had whittled down to a whip-lash,
Its twist of red and yellow lacquers
Sanded and polished,
And altogether so delicately wrought
That he had engraved his initials on it.

I last met Joseph Mary Plunkett Ward
In a pub just over the Irish border.
He was living in the open,
In a secret camp
On the other side of the mountain.
He was fighting for Ireland,
Making things happen.
And he told me, Joe Ward,
Of how he had risen through the ranks
To Quartermaster, Commandant:
How every morning at parade
His volunteers would call back *Anseo*
And raise their hands
As their names occurred.

Why Brownlee Left

Why Brownlee left, and where he went,
Is a mystery even now.
For if a man should have been content
It was him; two acres of barley,
One of potatoes, four bullocks,
A milker, a slated farmhouse.
He was last seen going out to plough
On a March morning, bright and early.

By noon Brownlee was famous;
They had found all abandoned, with
The last rig unbroken, his pair of black
Horses, like man and wife,
Shifting their weight from foot to
Foot, and gazing into the future.

Truce

It begins with one or two soldiers
And one or two following
With hampers over their shoulders.
They might be off wildfowling

As they would another Christmas Day,
So gingerly they pick their steps.
No one seems sure of what to do.
All stop when one stops.

A fire gets lit. Some spread
Their greatcoats on the frozen ground.
Polish vodka, fruit and bread
Are broken out and passed round.

The air of an old German song,
The rules of Patience, are the secrets
They'll share before long.
They draw on their last cigarettes

As Friday-night lovers, when it's over,
Might get up from their mattresses
To congratulate each other
And exchange names and addresses.

from QUOOF

Gathering Mushrooms

The rain comes flapping through the yard
like a tablecloth that she hand-embroidered.
My mother has left it on the line.
It is sodden with rain.
The mushroom shed is windowless, wide,
its high-stacked wooden trays
hosed down with formaldehyde.
And my father has opened the Gates of Troy
to that first load of horse manure.
Barley straw. Gypsum. Dried blood. Ammonia.
Wagon after wagon
blusters in, a self-renewing gold-black dragon
we push to the back of the mind.
We have taken our pitchforks to the wind.

All brought back to me that September evening
fifteen years on. The pair of us
tripping through Barnett's fair demesne
like girls in long dresses
after a hail-storm.
We might have been thinking of the fire-bomb
that sent Malone House sky-high
and its priceless collection of linen
sky-high.
We might have wept with Elizabeth McCrum.
We were thinking only of psilocybin.
You sang of the maid you met on the dewy grass –
And she stooped so low gave me to know
it was mushrooms she was gathering O.

He'll be wearing that same old donkey-jacket
and the sawn-off waders.
He carries a knife, two punnets, a bucket.
He reaches far into his own shadow.
We'll have taken him unawares
and stand behind him, slightly to one side.
He is one of those ancient warriors
before the rising tide.
He'll glance back from under his peaked cap
without breaking rhythm:
his coaxing a mushroom – a flat or a cup –
the nick against his right thumb;
the bucket then, the punnet to left or right,
and so on and so forth till kingdom come.

We followed the overgrown towpath by the Lagan.
The sunset would deepen through cinnamon
to aubergine,
the wood-pigeon's concerto for oboe and strings,
allegro, blowing your mind.
And you were suddenly out of my ken, hurtling
towards the ever-receding ground,
into the maw
of a shimmering green-gold dragon.
You discovered yourself in some outbuilding
with your long-lost companion, me,
though my head had grown into the head of a horse
that shook its dirty-fair mane
and spoke this verse:

Come back to us. However cold and raw, your feet
were always meant
to negotiate terms with bare cement.
Beyond this concrete wall is a wall of concrete
and barbed wire. Your only hope
is to come back. If sing you must, let your song
tell of treading your own dung,
let straw and dung give a spring to your step.
If we never live to see the day we leap
into our true domain,
lie down with us now and wrap
yourself in the soiled grey blanket of Irish rain
that will, one day, bleach itself white.
Lie down with us and wait.

The Sightseers

My father and mother, my brother and sister
and I, with uncle Pat, our dour best-loved uncle,
had set out that Sunday afternoon in July
in his broken-down Ford

not to visit some graveyard – one died of shingles,
one of fever, another's knees turned to jelly –
but the brand-new roundabout at Ballygawley,
the first in mid-Ulster.

Uncle Pat was telling us how the B-Specials
had stopped him one night somewhere near Ballygawley
and smashed his bicycle

and made him sing the Sash and curse the Pope of Rome.
They held a pistol so hard against his forehead
there was still the mark of an O when he got home.

Quoof

How often have I carried our family word
for the hot water bottle
to a strange bed,
as my father would juggle a red-hot half-brick
in an old sock
to his childhood settle.
I have taken it into so many lovely heads
or laid it between us like a sword.

A hotel room in New York City
with a girl who spoke hardly any English,
my hand on her breast
like the smouldering one-off spoor of the yeti
or some other shy beast
that has yet to enter the language.

The Frog

Comes to mind as another small upheaval
amongst the rubble.
His eye matches exactly the bubble
in my spirit-level.
I set aside hammer and chisel
and take him on the trowel.

The entire population of Ireland
springs from a pair left to stand
overnight in a pond
in the gardens of Trinity College,
two bottles of wine left there to chill
after the Act of Union.

There is, surely, in this story
a moral. A moral for our times.
What if I put him to my head
and squeezed it out of him,
like the juice of freshly squeezed limes,
or a lemon sorbet?

The More a Man Has
the More a Man Wants

At four in the morning he wakes
to the yawn of brakes,
the snore of a diesel engine.
Gone. All she left
is a froth of bra and panties.
The scum of the Seine
and the Farset.
Gallogly squats in his own pelt.
A sodium street light
has brought a new dimension
to their black taxi.
By the time they force an entry
he'll have skedaddled
among hen runs and pigeon lofts.

The charter flight from Florida
touched down at Aldergrove
minutes earlier,
at 3.54 a.m.
Its excess baggage takes the form
of Mangas Jones, Esquire,
who is, as it turns out, Apache.
He carries only hand luggage.
'Anything to declare?'
He opens the powder-blue attaché-
case. 'A pebble of quartz.'
'You're an Apache?' 'Mescalero.'
He follows the corridor's
arroyo till the signs read *Hertz*.

He is going to put his foot down
on a patch of waste ground
along the Stranmillis embankment
when he gets wind
of their impromptu fire.
The air above the once-sweet stream
is aquarium-
drained.
And six, maybe seven, skinheads
have formed a quorum
round a burnt-out heavy-duty tyre.
So intent on sniffing glue
they may not notice Gallogly,
or, if they do, are so far gone.

Three miles west as the crow flies
an all-night carry-out
provides the cover
for an illegal drinking club.
While the barman unpacks a crate
of Coca-Cola,
one cool customer
takes on all comers in a video game.
He grasps what his two acolytes
have failed to seize.
Don't they know what kind of take-away
this is, the glipes?
Vietmanese. Viet-ma-friggin'-*knees*.
He drops his payload of napalm.

Gallogly is wearing a candy-stripe
king-size sheet,
a little something he picked up
off a clothes line.
He is driving a milk van
he borrowed from the Belfast Co-op
while the milkman's back
was turned.
He had given the milkman a playful
rabbit punch.
When he stepped on the gas
he flooded the street
with broken glass.
He is trying to keep a low profile.

The unmarked police car draws level
with his last address.
A sergeant and eight constables
pile out of a tender
and hammer up the stairs.
The street bristles with static.
Their sniffer dog, a Labrador bitch,
bursts into the attic
like David Balfour in *Kidnapped*.
A constable on his first dawn swoop
leans on a shovel.
He has turned over a
new leaf in her ladyship's herb patch.
They'll take it back for analysis.

All a bit much after the night shift
to meet a milkman
who's double-parked his van
closing your front door after him.
He's sporting your
Donegal tweed suit and your
Sunday shoes and politely raises your
hat as he goes by.
You stand there with your mouth open
as he climbs into the still-warm
driving seat of your Cortina
and screeches off towards the motorway,
leaving you uncertain
of your still-warm wife's damp tuft.

Someone on their way to early Mass
will find her hog-tied
to the chapel gates –
O Child of Prague –
big-eyed, anorexic.
The lesson for today
is pinned to her bomber jacket.
It seems to read *Keep off the Grass*.
Her lovely head has been chopped
and changed.
For Beatrice, whose fathers
knew Louis Quinze,
to have come to this, her perruque
of tar and feathers.

He is pushing the maroon Cortina
through the sedge
on the banks of the Callan.
It took him a mere forty minutes
to skite up the M1.
He followed the exit sign
for Loughgall and hared
among the top-heavy apple orchards.
This stretch of the Armagh/Tyrone
border was planted by Warwickshiremen
who planted in turn
their familiar quick-set damson hedges.
The Cortina goes to the bottom.
Gallogly swallows a plummy-plum-plum.

'I'll warrant them's the very pair
o' boys I seen abroad
in McParland's bottom, though where
in under God –
for thou art so possessed with murd'rous hate –
where they come from God only knows.'
'They were mad for a bite o' mate,
I s'pose.'
'I doubt so. I come across a brave dale
o' half-chawed damsels. Wanst wun disappeared
I follied the wun as yelly as Indy male.'
'Ye weren't afeared?'
'I follied him.' 'God save us.'
'An' he driv away in a van belongin' t'*Avis*.'

The grass sprightly as Astroturf
in the September frost
and a mist
here where the ground is low.
He seizes his own wrist
as if, as if
Blind Pew again seized Jim
at the sign of the Admiral Benbow.
As if Jim Hawkins led Blind Pew
to Billy Bones
and they were all one and the same,
he stares in disbelief
at an aspirin-white spot he pressed
into his own palm.

Gallogly's thorn-proof tweed jacket
is now several sizes too big.
He has flopped
down in a hay shed
to ram a wad of hay into the toe
of each of his ill-fitting
brogues, when he gets the drift
of ham and eggs.
Now he's led by his own wet nose
to the hacienda-style
farmhouse, a baggy-kneed animated
bear drawn out of the woods
by an apple pie
left to cool on a windowsill.

She was standing at the picture window
with a glass of water
and a Valium
when she caught your man
in the reflection of her face.
He came
shaping past the milking parlour
as if he owned the place.
Such is the integrity
of their quarrel
that she immediately took down
the legally held shotgun
and let him have both barrels.
She had wanted only to clear the air.

Half a mile away across the valley
her husband's UDR patrol
is mounting a check-point.
He pricks up his ears
at the crack
of her prematurely arthritic hip-
joint,
and commandeers one of the jeeps.
There now, only a powder burn
as if her mascara had run.
The bloody puddle
in the yard, and the shilly-shally
of blood like a command wire
petering out behind a milk churn.

A hole in the heart, an ovarian
cyst.
Coming up the Bann
in a bubble.
Disappearing up his own bum.
Or, running on the spot
with all the minor aplomb
of a trick-cyclist.
So thin, side-on, you could spit
through him.
His six foot of pump water
bent double
in agony or laughter.
Keeping down-wind of everything.

White Annetts. Gillyflowers. Angel Bites.
When he names the forgotten names
of apples
he has them all off pat.
His eye like the eye of a travelling rat
lights on the studied negligence
of these scraws of turf.
A tarpaulin. A waterlogged pit.
He will take stock of the Kalashnikov's
filed-down serial number,
seven sticks of unstable
commercial gelignite
that have already begun to weep.
Red Strokes. Sugar Sweet. Widows Whelps.

Buy him a drink and he'll regale you
with how he came in for a cure
one morning after the night before
to the Las Vegas Lounge and Cabaret.
He was crossing the bar's
eternity of parquet floor
when his eagle eye
saw something move on the horizon.
If it wasn't an Indian.
A Sioux. An ugly Sioux.
He means, of course, an Oglala
Sioux busily tracing the family tree
of an Ulsterman who had some hand
in the massacre at Wounded Knee.

He will answer the hedge-sparrow's
Littlebitofbreadandnocheese
with a whole bunch
of freshly picked watercress,
a bulb of garlic,
sorrel,
with many-faceted blackberries.
Gallogly is out to lunch.
When his cock rattles its sabre
he takes it in his dab
hand, plants one chaste kiss
on its forelock,
and then, with a birl and a skirl,
tosses it off like a caber.

The UDR corporal had come off duty
to be with his wife
while the others set about
a follow-up search.
When he tramped out just before twelve
to exercise the greyhound
he was hit by a single high-velocity
shot.
You could, if you like, put your fist
in the exit wound
in his chest.
He slumps
in the spume of his own arterial blood
like an overturned paraffin lamp.

Gallogly lies down in the sheugh
to munch
through a Beauty of
Bath. He repeats himself, *Bath*,
under his garlic-breath.
Sheugh, he says. *Sheugh*.
He is finding that first 'sh'
increasingly difficult to manage.
Sh-leeps. A milkmaid sinks
her bare foot
to the ankle
in a simmering dung hill
and fills the slot
with beastlings for him to drink.

In Ovid's conspicuously tongue-in-cheek
account of an eyeball
to eyeball
between the goddess Leto
and a shower of Lycian reed cutters
who refuse her a cup of cloudy
water
from their churned-up lake,
Live then forever in that lake of yours,
she cries, and has them
bubble
and squeak
and plonk themselves down as bullfrogs
in their icy jissom.

A country man kneels on his cap
beside his neighbour's fresh
grave-mud
as Gallogly kneels to lap
the primrose-yellow
custard.
The knees of his hand-me-down duds
are gingerish.
A pernickety seven-
year-old girl-child
parades in her mother's trousseau
and mumbles a primrose
Kleenex tissue
to make sure her lipstick's even.

Gallogly has only to part the veil
of its stomach wall
to get right under the skin,
the spluttering heart
and collapsed lung,
of the horse in *Guernica*.
He flees the Museum of Modern Art
with its bit between his teeth.
When he began to cough
blood, Hamsun rode the Minneapolis/
New York night train
on top of the dining-car.
One long, inward howl.
A porter-drinker without a thrapple.

A weekend trip to the mountains
north of Boston
with Alice, Alice A.
and her paprika hair,
the ignition key
to her family's Winnebago camper,
her quim
biting the leg off her.
In the oyster bar
of Grand Central Station
she gobbles a dozen Chesapeakes –
'Oh, I'm not particular as to size' –
and, with a flourish of Tabasco,
turns to gobble him.

A brewery lorry on a routine delivery
is taking a slow,
dangerous bend.
The driver's blethering
his code name
over the Citizens' Band
when someone ambles
in front of him. Go, Johnny, go, go, go.
He's been dry-gulched
by a sixteen-year-old numb
with Mogadon,
whose face is masked by the seamless
black stocking filched
from his mum.

When who should walk in but Beatrice,
large as life, or larger,
sipping her one glass of lager
and singing her one song.
If he had it to do all over again
he would let her shave his head
in memory of '98
and her own, the French, Revolution.
The son of the King of the Moy
met this child on the Roxborough
estate. *Noblesse*, she said. *Noblesse
oblige*. And her tiny nipples
were bruise-bluish, wild raspberries.
The song she sang was 'The Croppy Boy'.

Her *grand-mère* was once asked to tea
by Gertrude Stein,
and her *grand-mère* and Gertrude
and Alice B., *chère* Alice B.
with her hook-nose,
the three of them sat in the nude
round the petits fours
and repeated *Eros is Eros is Eros.*
If he had it to do all over again
he would still be taken in
by her Alice B. Toklas
Nameless Cookies
and those new words she had him learn:
hash, hashish, *lo perfido assassin.*

Once the local councillor straps
himself into the safety belt
of his Citroën
and skids up the ramp
from the municipal car park
he upsets the delicate balance
of a mercury-tilt
boobytrap.
Once they collect his smithereens
he doesn't quite add up.
They're shy of a foot, and a calf
which stems
from his left shoe like a severely
pruned-back shrub.

Ten years before. The smooth-as-a-
front-lawn at Queen's
where she squats
before a psilocybin god.
The indomitable gentle-bush
that had Lanyon or Lynn
revise their elegant ground plan
for the university quad.
With calmness, with care,
with breast milk, with dew.
There's no cure now.
There's nothing left to do.
The mushrooms speak through her.
Hush-hush.

'Oh, I'm not particular as to size,'
Alice hastily replied
and broke off a bit of the edge
with each hand
and set to work very carefully,
nibbling
first at one
and then the other.
On the Staten Island Ferry
two men are dickering
over the price
of a shipment of Armalites,
as Henry Thoreau was wont to quibble
with Ralph Waldo Emerson.

That last night in the Algonquin
he met with a flurry
of sprites,
the assorted shades
of Wolfe Tone, Napper Tandy,
a sanguine
Michael Cusack
brandishing his blackthorn.
Then Thomas Meagher
darts up from the Missouri
on a ray
of the morning star
to fiercely ask
what has become of Irish hurling.

Everyone has heard the story of
a strong and beautiful bug
which came out of the dry leaf
of an old table of apple-tree wood
that stood
in a farmer's kitchen in Massachusetts
and which was heard gnawing out
for several weeks –
When the phone trills
he is careful not to lose his page –
Who knows what beautiful and winged life
whose egg
has been buried for ages
may unexpectedly come forth? 'Tell-tale.'

Gallogly carries a hunting bow
equipped
with a bow sight
and a quiver
of hunting arrows
belonging to her brother.
Alice has gone a little way off
to do her job.
A timber wolf,
a caribou,
or merely a trick of the light?
As, listlessly,
he lobs
an arrow into the undergrowth.

Had you followed the river Callan's
Pelorus Jack
through the worst drought
in living memory
to the rains of early autumn
when it scrubs its swollen,
scab-encrusted back
under a bridge, the bridge you look down from,
you would be unlikely to pay much heed
to yet another old banger
no one could be bothered to tax,
or a beat-up fridge
well-stocked with gelignite,
or some five hundred yards of Cortex.

He lopes after the dribs of blood
through the pine forest
till they stop dead
in the ruins of a longhouse
or hogan.
Somehow, he finds his way
back to their tent.
Not so much as a whiff of her musk.
The girl behind the Aer Lingus
check-in desk
at Logan
is wearing the same scent
and an embroidered capital letter *A*
on her breast.

Was she Aurora, or the goddess Flora,
Artemidora, or Venus bright,
or Helen fair beyond compare
that Priam stole from the Grecian sight?
Quite modestly she answered me
and she gave her head one fetch up
and she said I am gathering musheroons
to make my mammy ketchup.
The dunt and dunder
of a culvert-bomb
wakes him
as it might have woke Leander.
And she said I am gathering musheroons
to make my mammy ketchup O.

Predictable as the gift of the gab
or a drop of the craythur
he noses round the six-foot-deep
crater.
Oblivious to their Land Rover's
olive-drab
and the burgundy berets
of a snatch-squad of paratroopers.
Gallogly, or Gollogly,
otherwise known as Golightly,
otherwise known as Ingoldsby,
otherwise known as English,
gives forth one low cry of anguish
and agrees to come quietly.

They have bundled him into the cell
for a strip-
search.
He perches
on the balls of his toes, my my,
with his legs spread
till both his instep arches
fall.
He holds himself at arm's
length from the brilliantly Snowcem-ed
wall, a game bird
hung by its pinion tips
till it drops, in the fullness of time,
from the mast its colours are nailed to.

They have left him to cool his heels
after the obligatory
bath,
the mug shots, fingerprints
et cetera.
He plumps the thin bolster
and hints
at the slop bucket.
Six o'clock.
From the A Wing of Armagh jail
he can make out
the Angelus bell
of St Patrick's cathedral
and a chorus of 'For God and Ulster'.

The brewery lorry's stood at a list
by the Las Vegas
throughout the afternoon,
its off-side rear tyres down.
As yet, no one has looked agog
at the smuts and rusts
of a girlie mag
in disarray on the passenger seat.
An almost invisible, taut
fishing line
runs from the Playmate's navel
to a pivotal
beer keg.
As yet, no one has risen to the bait.

I saw no mountains, no enormous spaces,
no magical growth and metamorphosis
of buildings, nothing remotely like
a drama or a parable
in which he dons these lime-green
dungarees,
green Wellingtons,
a green helmet of aspect terrible.
The other world to which mescalin
admitted me was not the world of visions;
it existed out there, in what I could see
with my eyes open.
He straps a chemical pack on his back
and goes in search of some Gawain.

Gallogly pads along the block
to raise his visor
at the first peep-hole.
He shamelessly
takes in her lean piglet's
back, the back
and boyish hams
of a girl at stool.
At last. A tiny goat's-pill.
A stub of crayon
with which she has squiggled
a shamrock, yes,
but a shamrock after the school
of Pollock, Jackson Pollock.

I stopped and stared at her face to face
and on the spot a name came to me,
a name with a smooth, nervous sound:
Ylayali.
When she was very close
I drew myself up straight
and said in an impressive voice,
'Miss, you are losing your book.'
And Beatrice, for it is she, she squints
through the spy-hole
to pass him an orange,
an Outspan orange some visitor has spiked
with a syringe-ful
of vodka.

The more a man has the more a man wants,
the same I don't think true.
For I never met a man with one black eye
who ever wanted two.
In the Las Vegas Lounge and Cabaret
the resident group –
pot bellies, Aran knits –
have you eating out of their hands.
Never throw a brick at a drowning man
when you're near to a grocer's store.
Just throw him a cake of Sunlight soap,
let him wash himself ashore.
You will act the galoot, and gallivant,
and call for another encore.

Gallogly, Gallogly, O Gallogly
juggles
his name like an orange
between his outsize baseball glove
paws,
and ogles
a moon that's just out of range
beyond the perimeter wall.
He works a gobbet of Brylcreem
into his quiff
and delves
through sand and gravel,
shrugging it off
his velveteen shoulders and arms.

Just
throw
him
a
cake
of
Sunlight
soap,
let
him
wash
him-
self
ashore.

Into a picture by Edward Hopper
of a gas station
in the Midwest
where Hopper takes as his theme
light, the spooky
glow of an illuminated sign
reading Esso or Mobil
or what-have-you –
into such a desolate oval
ride two youths on a motorbike.
A hand gun. Balaclavas.
The pump attendant's grown so used
to hold-ups he calls after them:
Beannacht Dé ar an obair.

The pump attendant's not to know
he's being watched by a gallowglass
hot-foot from a woodcut
by Derricke,
who skips across the forecourt
and kicks the black
plastic bucket
they left as a memento.
Nor is the gallowglass any the wiser.
The bucket's packed with fertilizer
and a heady brew
of sugar and Paraquat's
relentlessly gnawing its way through
the floppy knot of a Durex.

It was this self-same pump attendant
who dragged the head and torso
clear
and mouthed an Act of Contrition
in the frazzled ear
and overheard
those already-famous last words
Moose . . . Indian.
'Next of all wus the han'.' 'Be Japers.'
'The sodgers cordonned off the area
wi' what-ye-may-call-it tape.'
'Lunimous.' 'They foun' this hairy
han' wi' a drowneded man's grip
on a lunimous stone no bigger than a . . .'

'Huh.'

from MEETING THE BRITISH

The Coney

Although I have never learned to mow
I suddenly found myself halfway through
last year's pea-sticks
and cauliflower-stalks
in our half-acre of garden.
My father had always left the whetstone
safely wrapped
in his old, tweed cap
and balanced on one particular plank
beside the septic tank.

This past winter he had been too ill
to work. The scythe would dull
so much more quickly in my hands
than his, and was so often honed
that while the blade
grew less and less a blade
the whetstone had entirely disappeared
and a lop-eared
coney was now curled inside the cap.
He whistled to me through the gap

in his front teeth;
'I was wondering, chief,
if you happen to know the name
of the cauliflowers in your cold-frame
that you still hope to dibble
in this unenviable
bit of ground?'
'They would be *All the Year Round.*'
'I guessed as much'; with that he swaggered
along the diving-board

and jumped. The moment he hit the water
he lost his tattered
bathing-togs
to the swimming-pool's pack of dogs.
'Come in'; this flayed
coney would parade
and pirouette like honey on a spoon:
'Come on in, Paddy Muldoon.'
And although I have never learned to swim
I would willingly have followed him.

Meeting the British

We met the British in the dead of winter.
The sky was lavender

and the snow lavender-blue.
I could hear, far below,

the sound of two streams coming together
(both were frozen over)

and, no less strange,
myself calling out in French

across that forest-
clearing. Neither General Jeffrey Amherst

nor Colonel Henry Bouquet
could stomach our willow-tobacco.

As for the unusual
scent when the Colonel shook out his hand-

kerchief: *C'est la lavande,
une fleur mauve comme le ciel.*

They gave us six fishhooks
and two blankets embroidered with smallpox.

Christo's

Two workmen were carrying a sheet of asbestos
down the Main Street of Dingle;
it must have been nailed, at a slight angle,
to the same-sized gap between Brandon

and whichever's the next mountain.
Nine o'clock. We watched the village dogs
take turns to spritz the hotel's refuse-sacks.
I remembered Tralee's unbiodegradable flags

from the time of the hunger-strikes.
We drove all day past mounds of sugar-beet,
hay-stacks, silage-pits, building-sites,
a thatched cottage even –

all of them draped in black polythene
and weighted against the north-east wind
by concrete blocks, old tyres; bags of sand
at a makeshift army post

across the border. By the time we got to Belfast
the whole of Ireland would be under wraps
like, as I said, 'one of your man's landscapes'.
'Your man's? You don't mean Christo's?'

The Fox

Such an alarm
as was raised last night
by the geese
on John Mackle's goose-farm.

I got up and opened
the venetian blind.
You lay
three fields away

in Collegelands
graveyard, in ground
so wet you weren't so much
buried there as drowned.

That was a month ago.
I see your face
above its bib
pumped full of formaldehyde.

You seem engrossed,
as if I'd come on you
painfully writing your name
with a carpenter's pencil

on the lid
of a mushroom-box.
You're saying, *Go back to bed.*
It's only yon dog-fox.

The Soap-Pig

I must have been dozing in the tub
when the telephone
rang and a small, white grub
crawled along the line
and into my head:
Michael Heffernan was dead.

All I could think of
was his Christmas present
from what must have been 1975.
It squatted there on the wash-stand,
an amber, pig-shaped
bar of soap.

He had breezed into Belfast
in a three-quarter-length coney-fur
to take up the post
of Drama Producer
with the still-reputable Beeb,
where I had somehow wangled a job.

Together we learned from Denys
Hawthorne and Allan McClelland
to float, like Saint Gennys,
on our own hands
through airwaves mostly jammed by cub
reporters and poisoned pups.

He liked to listen at full tilt
to bootleg tapes
of Ian Paisley's assaults
on Papes,
regretful only that they weren't in quad.
His favourite word was *quidditas*.

I could just see the Jesuitical,
kitsch-camp slip-
knot in the tail
of even that bar of soap.
For this was Heffernan
saying, 'You stink to high heaven.'

Which I well knew. Many's an Arts Club
night with Barfield and Mason
ended with me throwing up
at the basin.
Anne-Marie looked on, her unspoken,
'That's to wash, not boke in.'

This, or any, form of self-regard
cut no ice
with Michael, who'd undergone heart
surgery at least twice
while I knew him. On a trip
once to the Wexford slobs

he and I had shared
a hotel room. When he slipped
off his shirt
there were two unfashionably broad lap-
els where the surgeons had sawn
through the xylophone

on which he liked to play
Chopin or *Chop-*
sticks until he was blue
in the face; be-bop, doo-wop:
they'd given him a tiny, plastic valve
that would, it seemed, no more dissolve

than the soap-pig I carried
on successive flits
from Marlborough Park (and Anne-Marie)
to the Malone Avenue flat
(*Chez Moy*, it was later dubbed)
to the rented house in Dub (as in *Dub-*

lin) Lane,
until, at last, in Landseer Street
Mary unpeeled its cellophane
and it landed on its feet
among porcelain, glass and heliotrope
pigs from all parts of the globe.

When we went on holiday to France
our house-sitter was troub-
led by an unearthly fragrance
at one particular step
on the landing. It was no pooka,
of course, but the camomile soap-pig

that Mary, in a fit of pique,
would later fling into the back yard.
As I unpicked
the anthracite-shards
from its body, I glimpsed the scrab-
nosed, condemned slab

of our sow that dropped
dead from a chill in 1966,
its uneven litter individually wrapped
in a banana box
with polystyrene and wood-shavings;
this time Mary was leaving,

taking with her the gold
and silver pigs, the ivory.
For Michael Heffernan, the common cold
was an uncommon worry
that might as easily have stopped
him in his tracks. He'd long since escaped

Belfast for London's dog-eat-dog
back-stab
and leap-frog.
More than once he collap-
sed at his desk. But Margaret
would steady him through the Secretariat

towards their favourite restaurant
where, given my natural funk
I think of as restraint,
I might have avoided that Irish drunk
whose slow jibes
Michael parried, but whose quick jab

left him forever at a loss for words.
For how he would delib-
erate on whether two six-foot boards
sealed with ship's
varnish and two tea-chests
(another move) on which all this rests

is a table; or this merely a token
of some ur-chair,
or – being broken –
a chair at all: the mind's a razor
on the body's strop.
And the soap-pig? It's a bar of soap,

now the soap-sliver
in a flowered dish
that I work each morning into a lather
with my father's wobbling-brush,
then reconcile to its pool of glop
on my mother's wash-stand's marble top.

from MADOC: A MYSTERY

The Key

I ran into Foley six months ago in a dubbing suite in Los Angeles. He was halfway through post-production on a remake of *The Hoodlum Priest*, a film for which I've a special affection since my cousin Marina McCall was an extra in the first version. She had worked as a nanny for various movie stars, including Tippi Hedren, and seemed to spend half her time in the sky between New York and LA. Though I sat through three or four showings of *The Hoodlum Priest* in the Olympic Cinema, Moy, and carefully scrutinized the crowd scenes, I was never able to point to Marina with anything like conviction.

Foley was working on a sequence involving a police line-up, in which the victim shuffled along, stopped with each suspect in turn, then shuffled on. At a critical moment, she dropped a key on the floor. Foley was having trouble matching sound to picture on this last effect. I was struck by the fact that, just as early radio announcers had worn dinner-jackets, he was wearing an ultramarine tuxedo. After half a dozen attempts, he decided to call it quits, and emerged from his sound booth like a diver from a bathyscope. He offered me a tidbit that tasted only of mesquite.

I wanted to say something about Marina, something about an 'identity parade' in which I once took part, something about the etymology of 'tuxedo', but I found myself savouring the play between 'booth' and 'bathy-', 'quits' and 'mesquite', and began to 'misquote' myself:

When he sookied a calf down a boreen
it was through Indo-European.
When he clicked at a donkey carting dung
your grandfather had an African tongue.
You seem content to ventriloquize the surf.

Foley swallowed whatever it was:

Still defending that same old patch of turf?
Have you forgotten that 'hoodlum' is back-slang
for the leader of a San Francisco street-gang?

He flounced off into his cubicle. Though this, our only exchange, was remarkable for its banality, Foley has had some profound effect on me. These past six months I've sometimes run a little ahead of myself, but mostly I lag behind, my footfalls already pre-empted by their echoes.

Tea

I was rooting through tea-chest after tea-chest
as they drifted in along Key West

when I chanced on *Pythagoras in America*:
the book had fallen open at a book-mark

of tea; a tassel
of black watered silk from a Missal;

a tea-bird's black tail-feather.
All I have in the house is some left-over

squid cooked in its own ink
and this unfortunate cup of tea. Take it. Drink.

The Panther

For what it's worth, the last panther in Massachusetts
was brought to justice
in the woods beyond these meadows
and hung by its heels from a meat-hook
in what is now our kitchen.

(The house itself is something of a conundrum,
built as it was by an Ephraim Cowan from Antrim.)

I look in one evening while Jean
is jelly-making. She has rendered down pounds of grapes
and crab-apples
to a single jar
at once impenetrable and clear:
'Something's missing. This simply won't take.'

The air directly under the meat-hook –
it quakes, it quickens;
on a flagstone, the smudge of the tippy-tip of its nose.

Cauliflowers

Plants that glow in the dark have been developed through gene-splicing, in which light-producing bacteria from the mouths of fish are introduced to cabbage, carrots and potatoes.

The National Enquirer

More often than not he stops at the headrig to light
his pipe
and try to regain
his composure. The price of cauliflowers
has gone down
two weeks in a row on the Belfast market.

From here we can just make out
a platoon of Light
Infantry going down
the road to the accompaniment of a pipe-
band. The sun glints on their silver-
buttoned jerkins.

My uncle, Patrick Regan,
has been leaning against the mud-guard
of the lorry. He levers
open the bonnet and tinkers with a light
wrench at the hose-pipe
that's always going down.

Then he himself goes down
to bleed oil into a jerry-can.
My father slips the pipe
into his scorch-marked
breast pocket and again makes light
of the trepanned cauliflowers.

All this as I listened to lovers
repeatedly going down
on each other in the next room . . . 'light
of my life . . .' in a motel in Oregon.
All this. Magritte's
pipe

and the pipe-
bomb. White Annetts. Gillyflowers.
Margaret,
are you grieving? My father going down
the primrose path with Patrick Regan.
All gone out of the world of light.

All gone down
the original pipe. And the cauliflowers
in an unmarked pit, that were harvested by their own light.

The Briefcase

for Seamus Heaney

I held the briefcase at arm's length from me;
the oxblood or liver
eelskin with which it was covered
had suddenly grown supple.

I'd been waiting in line for the cross-town
bus when an almighty cloudburst
left the sidewalk a raging torrent.

And though it contained only the first
inkling of this poem, I knew I daren't
set the briefcase down
to slap my pockets for an obol –

for fear it might slink into a culvert
and strike out along the East River
for the sea. By which I mean the 'open' sea.

from THE ANNALS OF CHILE

Brazil

When my mother snapped open her flimsy parasol
it was Brazil: if not Brazil,

then Uruguay.
One nipple darkening her smock.

My shame-faced *Tantum Ergo*
struggling through thurified smoke.

*

Later that afternoon would find
me hunched over the font

as she rinsed my hair. Her towel-turban.
Her terrapin

comb scuttling under the faucet.
I stood there in my string vest

and shorts while she repeated, '*Champi . . . ?*
Champi . . . ? Champi . . . ?' Then,

that bracelet of shampoo
about the bone, her triumphant '*Champiñon*'.

*

If not Uruguay, then Ecuador:
it must be somewhere on or near the equator

given how water
plunged headlong into water

when she pulled the plug.
So much for the obliq-

uity of leaving *What a Boy Should Know*
under my pillow: now *vagina* and *vas*

deferens made a holy show
of themselves. 'There is inherent vice

in everything,' as O'Higgins
would proclaim: it was O'Higgins who duly

had the terms 'widdershins'
and 'deasil' expunged from the annals of Chile.

The Sonogram

Only a few weeks ago, the sonogram of Jean's womb
resembled nothing so much
as a satellite-map of Ireland;

now the image
is so well-defined we can make out not only a hand
but a thumb;

on the road to Spiddal, a woman hitching a ride;
a gladiator in his net, passing judgement on the crowd.

Footling

This I don't believe: rather than take a header
off the groyne
and into the ground-swell,
yea verily, the *ground-swell* of life,

she shows instead her utter
disregard – part diffidence, but mostly scorn –
for what lies behind the great sea-wall
and what knocks away at the great sea-cliff;

though she's been in training all spring and summer
and swathed herself in fat
and Saran-

Wrap like an old-time Channel swimmer,
she's now got cold feet
and turned in on herself, the phantom 'a' in Cesarian

The Birth

Seven o'clock. The seventh day of the seventh month of the
    year.
No sooner have I got myself up in lime-green scrubs,
a sterile cap and mask,
and taken my place at the head of the table

than the windlass-women ply their shears
and gralloch-grub
for a footling foot, then, warming to their task,
haul into the inestimable

realm of apple-blossoms and chanterelles and damsons and
    eel-spears
and foxes and the general hubbub
of inkies and jennets and Kickapoos with their lemniscs
or peekaboo-quiffs of Russian sable

and tallow-unctuous vernix, into the realm of the widgeon –
the 'whew' or 'yellow-poll', not the 'zuizin' –

Dorothy Aoife Korelitz Muldoon: I watch through floods of
    tears
as they give her a quick rub-a-dub
and whisk
her off to the nursery, then check their staple-guns for staples.

Incantata

In memory of Mary Farl Powers

I thought of you tonight, *a leanbh*, lying there in your long barrow
colder and dumber than a fish by Francisco de Herrera,
as I X-Actoed from a spud the Inca
glyph for a mouth: thought of that first time I saw your pink
spotted torso, distant-near as a nautilus,
when you undid your portfolio, yes indeedy,
and held the print of what looked like a cankered potato
at arm's length – your arms being longer, it seemed, than Lugh's.

Even Lugh of the Long (sometimes the Silver) Arm
would have wanted some distance between himself and the army-
   worms
that so clouded the sky over St Cloud you'd have to seal
the doors and windows and steel
yourself against their nightmarish *déjeuner sur l'herbe:*
try as you might to run a foil
across their tracks, it was to no avail;
the army-worms shinnied down the stove-pipe on an army-worm
   rope.

I can hardly believe that, when we met, my idea of 'R and R'
was to get smashed, almost every night, on sickly-sweet Demerara
rum and Coke: as well as leaving you a grass widow
(remember how Krapp looks up 'viduity'?),
after eight or ten or twelve of those dark rums
it might be eight or ten or twelve o'clock before I'd land
back home in Landseer Street, deaf and blind
to the fact that not only was I all at sea, but in the doldrums.

Again and again you'd hold forth on your own version of
    Thomism,
your own *Summa*
Theologiae that in everything there is an order,
that the things of the world sing out in a great oratorio:
it was Thomism, though, tempered by *La Nausée*,
by His Nibs Sam Bethicket,
and by that Dublin thing, that an artist must walk down Baggott
Street wearing a hair-shirt under the shirt of Nessus.

'*D'éirigh me ar maidin,*' I sang, '*a tharraingt chun aoinigh mhóir*':
our first night, you just had to let slip that your secret amour
for a friend of mine was such
that you'd ended up lying with him in a ditch
under a bit of whin, or gorse, or furze,
somewhere on the border of Leitrim, perhaps, or Roscommon:
'gamine', I wanted to say, 'kimono';
even then it was clear I'd never be at the centre of your universe.

Nor should I have been, since you were there already, your own
    Ding
an sich, no less likely to take wing
than the Christ you drew for a Christmas card as a pupa
in swaddling clothes: and how resolutely you would pooh pooh
the idea I shared with Vladimir and Estragon,
with whom I'd been having a couple of jars,
that this image of the Christ-child swaddled and laid in the
    manger
could be traced directly to those army-worm dragoons.

I thought of the night Vladimir was explaining to all and sundry
the difference between *geantrai* and *suantrai*
and you remarked on how you used to have a crush
on Burt Lancaster as Elmer Gantry, and Vladimir went to brush
the ash off his sleeve with a legerdemain
that meant only one thing – 'Why does he put up with this
    crap?' –
and you weighed in with 'To live in a dustbin, eating scrap,
seemed to Nagg and Nell a most eminent domain.'

How little you were exercised by those tiresome literary
    intrigues,
how you urged me to have no more truck
than the Thane of Calder
with a fourth estate that professes itself to be *'égalitaire'*
but wants only blood on the sand: yet, irony of ironies,
you were the one who, in the end,
got yourself up as a *retiarius* and, armed with net and trident,
marched from Mount Street to the Merrion Square arena.

In the end, you were the one who went forth to beard the lion,
you who took the DART line
every day from Jane's flat in Dun Laoghaire, or Dalkey,
dreaming your dream that the subterranean Dodder and Tolka
might again be heard above the *hoi polloi*
for whom Irish 'art' means a High Cross at Carndonagh or
    Corofin
and *The Book of Kells*: not until the lion cried craven
would the poor Tolka and the poor Dodder again sing out for joy.

I saw you again tonight, in your jump-suit, thin as a rake,
your hand moving in such a deliberate arc
as you ground a lithographic stone
that your hand and the stone blurred to one
and your face blurred into the face of your mother, Betty Wahl,
who took your failing, ink-stained hand
in her failing, ink-stained hand
and together you ground down that stone by sheer force of will.

I remember your pooh poohing, as we sat there on the
   'Enterprise',
my theory that if your name is Powers
you grow into it or, at least,
are less inclined to tremble before the likes of this bomb-blast
further up the track: I myself was shaking like a leaf
as we wondered whether the IRA or the Red
Hand Commandos or even the Red
Brigades had brought us to a standstill worthy of Hamm and
   Clov.

Hamm and Clov; Nagg and Nell; Watt and Knott;
the fact is that we'd been at a standstill long before the night
things came to a head,
long before we'd sat for half the day in the sweltering heat
somewhere just south of Killnasaggart
and I let slip a name – her name – off my tongue
and you turned away (I see it now) the better to deliver the sting
in your own tail, to let slip your own little secret.

I thought of you again tonight, thin as a rake, as you bent
over the copper plate of 'Emblements',
its tidal wave of army-worms into which you all but
     disappeared:
I wanted to catch something of its spirit
and yours, to body out your disembodied *vox
clamantis in deserto*, to let this all-too-cumbersome device
of a potato-mouth in a potato-face
speak out, unencumbered, from its long, low, mould-filled box.

I wanted it to speak to what seems always true of the truly
     great,
that you had a winningly inaccurate
sense of your own worth, that you would second-guess
yourself too readily by far, that you would rally to any cause
before your own, mine even,
though you detected in me a tendency to put
on too much artificiality, both as man and poet,
which is why you called me 'Polyester' or 'Polyurethane'.

That last time in Dublin, I copied with a quill dipped in oak-
     gall
onto a sheet of vellum, or maybe a human caul,
a poem for *The Great Book of Ireland*: as I watched the low
swoop over the lawn today of a swallow
I thought of your animated talk of Camille Pissarro
and André Derain's *The Turning Road, L'Estaque*:
when I saw in that swallow's nest a face in a mud-pack
from that muddy road I was filled again with a profound sorrow.

You must have known already, as we moved from the 'Hurly
   Burly'
to McDaid's or Riley's,
that something was amiss: I think you even mentioned a
   homeopath
as you showed off the great new acid-bath
in the Graphic Studio, and again undid your portfolio
to lay out your latest works; I try to imagine the strain
you must have been under, pretending to be as right as rain
while hearing the bells of a church from some long-flooded valley.

From the Quabbin reservoir, maybe, where the banks and
   bakeries
of a dozen little submerged Pompeii reliquaries
still do a roaring trade: as clearly as I saw your death-mask
in that swallow's nest, you must have heard the music
rise from the muddy ground between
your breasts as a nocturne, maybe, by John Field;
to think that you thought yourself so invulnerable, so inviolate,
that a little cancer could be beaten.

You must have known, as we walked through the ankle-deep
   clabber
with Katherine and Jean and the long-winded Quintus Calaber,
that cancer had already made such a breach
that you would almost surely perish:
you must have thought, as we walked through the woods
along the edge of the Quabbin,
that rather than let some doctor cut you open
you'd rely on infusions of hardock, hemlock, all the idle weeds.

I thought again of how art may be made, as it was by André
    Derain,
of nothing more than a turn
in the road where a swallow dips into the mire
or plucks a strand of bloody wool from a strand of barbed wire
in the aftermath of Chickamauga or Culloden
and builds from pain, from misery, from a deep-seated hurt,
a monument to the human heart
that shines like a golden dome among roofs rain-glazed and
    leaden.

I wanted the mouth in this potato-cut
to be heard far beyond the leaden, rain-glazed roofs of Quito,
to be heard all the way from the southern hemisphere
to Clontarf or Clondalkin, to wherever your sweet-severe
spirit might still find a toe-hold
in this world: it struck me then how you would be aghast
at the thought of my thinking you were some kind of ghost
who might still roam the earth in search of an earthly delight.

You'd be aghast at the idea of your spirit hanging over this vale
of tears like a jump-suited jump-jet whose vapour-trail
unravels a sky: for there's nothing, you'd say, nothing over
and above the sky itself, nothing but cloud-cover
reflected in a thousand lakes; it seems that Minne-
sota itself means 'sky-tinted water', that the sky is a great slab
of granite or iron ore that might at any moment slip
back into the worked-out sky-quarry, into the worked-out sky-
    mines.

To use the word 'might' is to betray you once too often, to betray
your notion that nothing's random, nothing arbitrary:
the gelignite weeps, the hands fly by on the alarm clock,
the 'Enterprise' goes clackety-clack
as they all must; even the car hijacked that morning in the Cross,
that was preordained, its owner spread on the bonnet
before being gagged and bound or bound
and gagged, that was fixed like the stars in the Southern Cross.

The fact that you were determined to cut yourself off in your
    prime
because it was *pre*-determined has my eyes abrim:
I crouch with Belacqua
and Lucky and Pozzo in the Acacacac-
ademy of Anthropopopometry, trying to make sense of the
    '*quaquaqua*'
of that potato-mouth; that mouth as prim
and proper as it's full of self-opprobrium,
with its '*quaquaqua*', with its 'Quoiquoiquoiquoiquoiquoiquoiq'.

That's all that's left of the voice of Enrico Caruso
from all that's left of an opera-house somewhere in Matto Grosso,
all that's left of the hogweed and horehound and cuckoo-pint,
of the eighteen soldiers dead at Warrenpoint,
of the Black Church clique and the Graphic Studio claque,
of the many moons of glasses on a tray,
of the brewery-carts drawn by moon-booted drays,
of those jump-suits worn under your bottle-green worsted cloak.

Of the great big dishes of chicken lo mein and beef chow mein,
of what's mine is yours and what's yours mine,
of the oxlips and cowslips
on the banks of the Liffey at Leixlip
where the salmon breaks through the either/or neither/nor
  nether
reaches despite the temple-veil
of itself being rent and the penny left out overnight on the rail
is a sheet of copper when the mail-train has passed over.

Of the bride carried over the threshold, hey, only to alight
on the limestone slab of another threshold,
of the swarm, the cast,
the colt, the spew of bees hanging like a bottle of Lucozade
from a branch the groom must sever,
of Emily Post's ruling, in *Etiquette*,
on how best to deal with the butler being in cahoots
with the cook when they're both in cahoots with the chauffeur.

Of that poplar-flanked stretch of road between Leiden
and The Hague, of the road between Rathmullen and Ramelton,
where we looked so long and hard
for some trace of Spinoza or Amelia Earhart,
both of them going down with their engines on fire:
of the stretch of road somewhere near Urney
where Orpheus was again overwhelmed by that urge to turn
back and lost not only Eurydice but his steel-strung lyre.

Of the sparrows and finches in their bell of suet,
of the bitter-sweet
bottle of Calvados we felt obliged to open
somewhere near Falaise, so as to toast our new-found *copains*,
of the priest of the parish
who came enquiring about our 'status', of the hedge-clippers
I somehow had to hand, of him running like the clappers
up Landseer Street, of my subsequent self-reproach.

Of the remnants of Airey Neave, of the remnants of
    Mountbatten,
of the famous *andouilles*, of the famous *boudins*
noirs et blancs, of the barrel-vault
of the cathedral at Rouen, of the flashlight, fat and roll of felt
on each of their sledges, of the music
of Joseph Beuys's pack of huskies, of that baldy little bugger
mushing them all the way from Berncastel through Bacarrat
to Belfast, his head stuck with honey and gold-leaf like a
    mosque.

Of Benjamin Britten's *Lachrymae*, with its gut-wrenching viola,
of Vivaldi's *Four Seasons*, of Frankie Valli's,
of Braque's great painting *The Shower of Rain*,
of the fizzy, lemon or sherbet-green *Ranus ranus*
plonked down in Trinity like a little Naugahyde pouffe,
of eighteen soldiers dead in Oriel,
of the weakness for a little fol-de-rol-de-rolly
suggested by the gap between the front teeth of the Wife of
    Bath.

Of *A Sunday Afternoon on the Island of La Grande Jatte*, of
　Seurat's
piling of tesserae upon tesserae
to give us a monkey arching its back
and the smoke arching out from a smoke-stack,
of Sunday afternoons in the Botanic Gardens, going with the flow
of the burghers of Sandy Row and Donegal
Pass and Andersonstown and Rathcoole,
of the army Land Rover flaunt-flouncing by with its heavy
　furbelow.

Of Marlborough Park, of Notting Hill, of the Fitzroy Avenue
immortalized by Van 'His real name's Ivan'
Morrison, 'and him the dead spit
of Padraic Fiacc', of John Hewitt, the famous expat,
in whose memory they offer every year six of their best milch
　cows,
of the Bard of Ballymacarrett,
of every ungodly poet in his or her godly garret,
of Medhbh and Michael and Frank and Ciaran and 'wee' John
　Qughes.

Of the Belfast school, so called, of the school of hard knocks,
of your fervent eschewal of stockings and socks
as you set out to hunt down your foes
as implacably as the *tóraidheacht* through the Fews
of Redmond O'Hanlon, of how that 'd' and that 'c' aspirate
in *tóraidheacht* make it sound like a last gasp in an oxygen-tent,
of your refusal to open a vent
but to breathe in spirit of salt, the mordant salt-spirit.

Of how mordantly hydrochloric acid must have scored and
     scarred,
of the claim that boiled skirrets
can cure the spitting of blood, of that dank
flat somewhere off Morehampton Road, of the unbelievable
     stink
of valerian or feverfew simmering over a low heat,
of your sitting there, pale and gaunt,
with that great prescriber of boiled skirrets, Dr John Arbuthnot,
your face in a bowl of feverfew, a towel over your head.

Of the great roll of paper like a bolt of cloth
running out again and again like a road at the edge of a cliff,
of how you called a Red Admiral a Red
Admirable, of how you were never in the red
on either the first or the last
of the month, of your habit of loosing the drawstring of your
     purse
and finding one scrunched-up, obstreperous
note and smoothing it out and holding it up, pristine and
     pellucid.

Of how you spent your whole life with your back to the wall,
of your generosity when all the while
you yourself lived from hand
to mouth, of Joseph Beuys's pack of hounds
crying out from their felt and fat 'Atone, atone, atone',
of Watt remembering the 'Krak! Krek! Krik!'
of those three frogs' karaoke
like the still, sad *basso continuo* of the great quotidian.

Of a ground bass of sadness, yes, but also a sennet of hautboys
as the fat and felt hounds of Beuys O'Beuys
bayed at the moon over a caravan
in Dunmore East, I'm pretty sure it was, or Dungarvan:
of my guest appearance in your self-portrait not as a hidalgo
from a long line
of hidalgos but a hound-dog, a *leanbh*,
a dog that skulks in the background, a dog that skulks and stalks.

Of that self-portrait, of the self-portraits by Rembrandt van Rijn,
of all that's revelation, all that's rune,
of all that's composed, all composed of odds and ends,
of that daft urge to make amends
when it's far too late, too late even to make sense of the clutter
of false trails and reversed horseshoe tracks
and the aniseed we took it in turn to drag
across each other's scents, when only a fish is dumber and
    colder.

Of your avoidance of canned goods, in the main,
on account of the exceeeeeeeeeeeeeeeeedingly high risk of
    ptomaine,
of corned beef in particular being full of crap,
of your delight, so, in eating a banana as ceremoniously as
    Krapp
but flinging the skin over your shoulder like a thrush
flinging off a shell from which it's only just managed to disinter
a snail, like a stone-faced, twelfth-century
FitzKrapp eating his banana by the mellow, yellow light of a
    rush.

Of the 'Yes, let's go' spoken by Monsieur Tarragon,
of the early-ripening jardonelle, the tumorous jardon, the jargon
of jays, the jars
of tomato relish and the jars
of Victoria plums, absolutely *de rigueur* for a passable plum baba,
of the drawers full of balls of twine and butcher's string,
of Dire Straits playing 'The Sultans of Swing',
of the horse's hock suddenly erupting in those boils and buboes.

Of the Greek figurine of a pig, of the pig on a terracotta frieze,
of the sow dropping dead from some mysterious virus,
of your predilection for gammon
served with a sauce of coriander or cumin,
of the slippery elm, of the hornbeam or witch-, or even wych-,
hazel that's good for stopping a haemor-
rhage in mid-flow, of the merest of mere
hints of elderberry curing everything from sciatica to a stitch.

Of the decree *condemnator*, the decree *absolvitor*, the decree *nisi*,
of *Aosdána*, of *an chraobh cnuais*,
of the fields of buckwheat
taken over by garget, inkberry, scoke – all names for pokeweed –
of *Mother Courage*, of *Arturo Ui*,
of those Sunday mornings spent picking at sesame
noodles and all sorts and conditions of dim sum,
of tea and ham sandwiches in the Nesbitt Arms hotel in Ardara.

Of the day your father came to call, of your leaving your sick-
    room
in what can only have been a state of delirium,
of how you simply wouldn't relent
from your vision of a blind
watch-maker, of your fatal belief that fate
governs everything from the honey-rust of your father's terrier's
eyebrows to the horse that rusts and rears
in the furrow, of the furrows from which we can no more deviate

than they can from themselves, no more than the map of Europe
can be redrawn, than that Hermes might make a harp from his
    harpe,
than that we must live in a vale
of tears on the banks of the Lagan or the Foyle,
than that what we have is a done deal,
than that the Irish Hermes,
Lugh, might have leafed through his vast herbarium
for the leaf that had it within it, Mary, to anoint and anneal,

than that Lugh of the Long Arm might have found in the midst
    of *lus*
na leac or *lus na treatha* or *Frannc-lus*,
in the midst of eyebright, or speedwell, or tansy, an antidote,
than that this *Incantata*
might have you look up from your plate of copper or zinc
on which you've etched the row upon row
of army-worms, than that you might reach out, arrah,
and take in your ink-stained hands my own hands stained with
    ink.

from HAY

Lag

We were joined at the hip. We were joined at the hip
like some latter-day Chang and Eng,
though I lay in that dreadful kip
in North Carolina while you preferred to hang

loose in London, in that selfsame
'room in Bayswater'. You wrapped yourself in a flag
(the red flag, with a white elephant, of Siam)
and contemplated the time lag.

It was Chang, I seem to recall, who tried to choke
Eng when he'd had one over the eight.
It was Chang whose breath was always so sickly-sour.

It was Chang who suffered a stroke.
Eng was forced to shoulder his weight.
It was Chang who died first. Eng lived on for five hours.

Symposium

You can lead a horse to water but you can't make it hold
its nose to the grindstone and hunt with the hounds.
Every dog has a stitch in time. Two heads? You've been sold
one good turn. One good turn deserves a bird in the hand.

A bird in the hand is better than no bread.
To have your cake is to pay Paul.
Make hay while you can still hit the nail on the head.
For want of a nail the sky might fall.

People in glass houses can't see the wood
for the new broom. Rome wasn't built between two stools.
Empty vessels wait for no man.

A hair of the dog is a friend indeed.
There's no fool like the fool
who's shot his bolt. There's no smoke after the horse is gone.

Hay

This much I know. Just as I'm about to make that right turn
off Province Line Road
I meet another beat-up Volvo
carrying a load

of hay. (More accurately, a bale of lucerne
on the roof rack,
a bale of lucerne or fescue or alfalfa.)
My hands are raw. I'm itching to cut the twine, to unpack

that hay-accordion, that hay-concertina.
It must be ten o'clock. There's still enough light
(not least from the glow

of the bales themselves) for a body to ascertain
that when one bursts, as now, something takes flight
from those hot-and-heavy box pleats. This much, at least,
  I know.

Long Finish

Ten years since we were married, since we stood
under a chuppah of pine boughs
in the middle of a little pinewood
and exchanged our wedding vows.
Save me, good thou,
a piece of marchpane, while I fill your glass with Simi
Chardonnay as high as decency allows,
and then some.

Bear with me now as I myself must bear
the scrutiny of a bottle of wine
that boasts of hints of plum and pear,
its muscadine
tempered by an oak backbone. I myself have designs
on the willow-boss
of your breast, on all your waist confines
between longing and loss.

The wonder is that we somehow have withstood
the soars and slumps in the Dow
of ten years of marriage and parenthood,
its summits and its sloughs –
that we've somehow
managed to withstand an almond-blossomy
five years of bitter rapture, five of blissful rows
(and then some

if we count the one or two to spare
when we've been firmly on cloud nine).
Even now, as you turn away from me with your one bare
shoulder, the veer of your neckline,
I glimpse the all-but-cleared-up eczema patch on your spine
and it brings to mind not the Schloss
that stands, transitory, tra la, Triestine,
between longing and loss

but a crude
hip trench in a field, covered with pine boughs,
in which two men in masks and hoods
who have themselves taken vows
wait for a farmer to break a bale for his cows
before opening fire with semi-
automatics, cutting him off slightly above the eyebrows,
and then some.

It brings to mind another, driving out to care
for six white-faced kine
finishing on heather and mountain air,
another who'll shortly divine
the precise whereabouts of a land mine
on the road between Beragh and Sixmilecross,
who'll shortly know what it is to have breasted the line
between longing and loss.

Such forbearance in the face of vicissitude
also brings to mind the little 'there, theres' and 'now, nows'
of two sisters whose sleeves are imbued
with the constant douse and souse
of salt water through their salt house
in *Matsukaze* (or *Pining Wind*), by Zeami,
the salt house through which the wind soughs and soughs,
and then some

of the wind's little 'now, nows' and 'there, theres'
seem to intertwine
with those of Pining Wind and Autumn Rain, who must
    forbear
the dolour of their lives of boiling down brine.
For the double meaning of 'pine'
is much the same in Japanese as English, coming across
both in the sense of 'tree' and the sense we assign
between 'longing' and 'loss'

as when the ghost of Yukihira, the poet-courtier who wooed
both sisters, appears as a ghostly pine, pining among pine
    boughs.
Barely have Autumn Rain and Pining Wind renewed
their vows
than you turn back toward me, and your blouse,
while it covers the all-but-cleared-up patch of eczema,
falls as low as decency allows,
and then some.

Princess of Accutane, let's no more try to refine
the pure drop from the dross
than distinguish, good thou, between mine and thine,
between longing and loss,
but rouse
ourselves each dawn, here on the shore at Suma,
with such force and fervour as spouses may yet espouse,
and then some.

Errata

For 'Antrim' read 'Armagh'.
For 'mother' read 'other'.
For 'harm' read 'farm'.
For 'feather' read 'father'.

For 'Moncrieff' read 'Monteith'.
For *'Beal Fierste'* read *'Beal Feirste'*.
For 'brave' read 'grave'.
For 'revered' read 'reversed'.

For 'married' read 'marred'.
For 'pull' read 'pall'.
For 'ban' read 'bar'.
For 'smell' read 'small'.

For 'spike' read 'spoke'.
For 'lost' read 'last'.
For 'Steinbeck' read 'Steenbeck'.
For 'ludic' read 'lucid'.

For 'religion' read 'region'.
For 'ode' read code'.
For 'Jane' read 'Jean'.
For 'rod' read 'road'.

For 'pharoah' read 'pharoh'.
For *'Fíor-Gael'* read *'Fíor-Ghael'*.
For 'Jeffrey' read 'Jeffery'.
For 'vigil' read 'Virgil'.

For 'flageolet' read 'fava'.
For 'veto' read 'vote'.
For 'Aiofe' read 'Aoife'.
For 'anecdote' read 'antidote'.

For 'Rosemont' read 'Mount Rose'.
For 'plump' read 'plumb'.
For 'hearse' read 'hears'.
For 'loom' read 'bloom'.

from MOY SAND AND GRAVEL

Moy Sand and Gravel

To come out of the Olympic Cinema and be taken aback
by how, in the time it took a dolly to travel
along its little track
to the point where two movie stars' heads
had come together smackety-smack
and their kiss filled the whole screen,

those two great towers directly across the road
at Moy Sand and Gravel
had already washed, at least once, what had flowed
or been dredged from the Blackwater's bed
and were washing it again, load by load,
as if washing might make it clean.

A Collegelands Catechism

Which is known as the 'Orchard County'?
Which as the 'Garden State'?
Which captain of the *Bounty*
was set adrift by his mate?

Who cooked and ate an omelette
midway across Niagara Falls?
Where did Setanta get
those magical hurley balls

he ram-stammed down the throat
of the blacksmith's hound?
Why would a Greek philosopher of note
refuse to be bound

by convention but live in a tub
from which he might overhear,
as he went to rub
an apple on his sleeve, the mutineers

plotting to seize the *Maid of the Mist*
while it was still half-able to forge
ahead and make half a fist
of crossing the Niagara gorge,

the tub in which he might light a stove
and fold the beaten
eggs into themselves? Who unearthed the egg-trove?
And who, having eaten

the omelette, would marvel at how the Mounties
had so quickly closed in on him, late
of the 'Orchard County'
by way of the 'Garden State'?

The Loaf

When I put my finger to the hole they've cut for a dimmer
  switch
in a wall of plaster stiffened with horsehair
it seems I've scratched a two-hundred-year-old itch

with a pink and a pink and a pinkie-pick.

When I put my ear to the hole I'm suddenly aware
of spades and shovels turning up the gain
all the way from Raritan to the Delaware

with a clink and a clink and a clinky-click.

When I put my nose to the hole I smell the flood-plain
of the canal after a hurricane
and the spots of green grass where thousands of Irish have lain

with a stink and a stink and a stinky-stick.

When I put my eye to the hole I see one holding horse dung to
  the rain
in the hope, indeed, indeed,
of washing out a few whole ears of grain

with a wink and a wink and a winkie-wick.

And when I do at last succeed
in putting my mouth to the horsehair-fringed niche
I can taste the small loaf of bread he baked from that whole seed

with a link and a link and a linky-lick.

Redknots

The day our son is due is the very day
the redknots are meant to touch down
on their long haul
from Chile to the Arctic Circle,
where they'll nest on the tundra
within a few feet
of where they were hatched.
Forty or fifty thousand of them
are meant to drop in along Delaware Bay.

They time their arrival on these shores
to coincide with the horseshoe crabs
laying their eggs in the sand.
Smallish birds to begin with,
the redknots have now lost half their weight.
Eating the eggs of the horseshoe crabs
is what gives them the strength to go on,
forty or fifty thousand of them getting up all at once
as if for a rock concert encore.

At the Sign of the Black Horse, September 1999

Awesome, the morning after Hurricane Floyd, to sit out in
  our driveway and gawk
at yet another canoe or kayak
coming down Canal Road, now under ten feet of water. We've
  wheeled to the brim
the old Biltrite pram
in which, wrapped in a shawl of Carrickmacross
lace and a bonnet
of his great-grandmother Sophie's finest needlepoint,
Asher sleeps on, as likely as any of us to find a way across

the millrace on which logs (trees more than logs)
are borne along, to which the houses down by the old
  Griggstown Locks
have given up their inventory.
I'm happy for once to be left high and dry,
happy that the house I may yet bring myself to call mine
is set on a two-hundred-and-fifty-year-old slab,
happy that, if need be, we might bundle a few belongings into
  a pillow slip
and climb the hill and escape, Please Examine

Your Change, to a place where the soul might indeed recover
radical innocence. A police launch manoeuvring by brought
  back troops on manoeuvre,
some child-kin of my children dipping a stale
crust in his bowl of kale
while listening to his parents complain about the cost

of running a household
in the Poland of the 1930s, the child who, Please Hold,
a peaked cap would shortly accost

for the whereabouts of his uncle, the sofer.
Awesome, however stormy yesterday's weather, to calmly don
    a safari
hat that somewhat matches my safari coat
and, determined as I am to make the most of the power cut
here on Ararat,
tear another leaf from Edward Bulwer-Lytton's
King Poppy to light the barbecue, the barbecue shortly to be
    laden
with Dorothy's favourite medallions of young rat

and white-lipped peccary taken this morning not with old-
    fashioned piano wire
but the latest in traps. I'll rake the ashes of the fire
on which they'll cook, No Turn
On Red, and watch the Mediterranean
do its level best to meet the 'Caribbon',
as Dorothy pronounced it once, on Canal Road, No Way Out,
having taken down from the attic the ancient Underwood
with the one remaining black ribbon

and set up shop in a corner of the garage.
When we wheeled the old Biltrite baby carriage
to the brink this morning, I was awestruck to see in Asher's
    glabrous
face a slew of interlopers

not from Maghery, as I might have expected, or Maghera, or
  Magherafelt
(though my connections there are now few and far between),
but the likes of that kale-eating child on whom the peaked
  cap, *Verboten*,
would shortly pin a star of yellow felt,

having accosted him on the Mosaic
proscription, Please Secure Your Own Oxygen Mask
Before Attending To Children, on the eating of white-lipped
  peccary.
Just one step ahead of the police launch, meanwhile, a 1920
  Studebaker
had come down Canal Road, Do Not Fill
Above This Line, carrying another relative, Arnold Rothstein,
  the brain
behind the running, during Prohibition, of grain
alcohol into the States, his shirt the very same Day-Glo green
  of chlorophyll

on the surface of a cattle bath
or the canal itself, the canal that ordinarily reflects berm bank
  and towpath
as calm as calm. Jean had been fixing Asher a little gruel
from leftover cereal
and crumbled Zwieback
when Uncle Arnie came floating by the 'nursery'.
This was the Arnold Rothstein who had himself fixed the 1919
  World Series
by bribing eight Chicago White Sox players, Keep Back

Fifty Feet, to throw the game. So awestruck were we by his
  Day-Glo
shirt we barely noticed how low
in the water his Studebaker lay, the distribution of its cargo of
  grain alcohol
(filtered through a makeshift charcoal-
packed, double downspout
by an accomplice, Waxey Gordon) somewhat less than even.
'The peccary's hind foot,' the peaked cap would enquire, 'you
  call that *cloven*?'
Asher slept on, his little pout

set off beautifully by the pillow case
into which we might yet bundle the foul madams, the
  couscous,
the tabouleh carry-out
full of grit
from the Sahara, while Uncle Arnie had taken his lawyer's
  advice,
maintaining that he paid none of the eight White Sox
who stood in the witness box
as much as a nickel. Racketeering, maybe. Extortion, maybe.
  Maybe vice.

But not throwing games. It wasn't an area in which he had
  expertise. Not an expert.
Isaac Wolf of New Haven, meanwhile, had unzippered
a freezer bag and made a dent
in the defrosted dough in which we'd meant
to wrap the loin of peccary, Please Use Tongs,

in an Aussie version of the secret
recipe the Duke of Wellington had secured
from the Killadar of Perinda, one which substituted quantongs

for apricots. While Asher slept on, half hid
under the cradle hood,
his great-grandfather Jim Zabin, an ad-man who held, of all
    things, the Biltrite account,
Please Examine Your Change As Mistakes Cannot,
nodded from his death-bed to the red
stain on the muslin cloth
that covered the peccary in its autoclave
as if that cloth were an obstacle whereby the haystack- and
    roof-levelling wind, bred

on the Atlantic, might at last
be stayed. 'By which authority,' another great-grandfather,
    Sam Korelitz, would blast
from his hardware store in Lawrence, Mass., 'did you deny
    Asher a bris?'
A chainsaw had let rip. Our next-door neighbour, Bruce,
was making quite a hand
of amputating a sycamore limb that had given its all
to the wind and rain. Asher slept on, his shawl
of Carrickmacross lace, his bonnet tied with silk reputed to
    come from Samarkhand,

while Dorothy stood where the Delaware and Raritan Canal
    and the Millstone
River combined to carry tonne upon tonne

of clay, hay, hair, shoes, spectacles, Please Use The Hammer
   To Break
The Glass, playing ducks and drakes
with the child-kin shortly to be riven
from her family and I, the so-called Goy from the Moy,
scrubbed the trap made in Marengo, Illinois,
by which we took that white-lipped peccary, as if scrubbing
   might leave me shriven.

A flicker from behind Asher's sleeping lids, all covered with
   little wheals and whelks,
as Jean's distant cousin, Helene Hanff, began to rub a mix of
   cumin and baby talc
(cornstarch more than talc) into another loin
of peccary, this being a trick Helene
had picked up from the individual who started a trend
by keeping a rabbit warren-
cum-dovecote in a mews off Charing Cross Road, Hard Hats
   Must Be Worn,
an individual who picked it up from whichever Waugh
   deemed a pram in the hallway the end

of art, a Waugh who could no doubt trace it back to
   Wellington and the Killadar
of Perinda. I looked up in dismay as the helter-skelter
I'd raised in lieu of a lonely tower (part float, part floating
   derrick)
was nudged by the millrace. The increasingly eccentric
Helene, meanwhile, continued to rub
cornstarch into the remains

of whatever curled in the autoclave. Almost inaudible now,
  the sycamore moans
as, almost inaudibly, I myself continued to scrub

the latest in traps with a wire brush
from Sam's hardware store in Lawrence, Mass. 'You ignore
  the Midrash
by which authority?' I could hear small incendiary
devices going off in the midst of the pleasantries
exchanged at this, as every, family gathering, Please Do Not
  Leave Window Ajar,
where the stricken
face of Uncle Arnie's friend Fanny Brice peeked from her
  astrakhan.
'According to Horace,' Arnie maintained, 'every water
  pitcher started out as a wine jar.

You may take Fanny for a nincompoop,
but I fear she may well be the only one here who's actually
  read *King Poppy*.
I fear, moreover, the way the smoke flings
and flails itself from your barbecue brings back that terrible
  morning, in Sing Sing,
they fried Charlie Becker.' Helene looked up from her cumin
splitting while Bruce began to pulverize
a stand of young sassafras
with all the zeal of a chainsaw catechumen

and the groundbreaking Irish navvies continued to keen and
  kvetch

through the hole cut for a dimmer switch
in a wall of deh-dah stiffened with deh-dah. Next to moor
his little punt at our dock was Joe Hanff, the banker who
    helped Louis B. Mayer
and Thomas Edison develop a 'cool' projection lamp. Where
    he'd come by the Coke and bucket
of popcorn God only knows.
He handed them to Dorothy for safekeeping while he
    concentrated on the minutiae
of the peccary trap and the great trebucket

with which we've been known to take even larger critters,
setting and upsetting the trebucket as would an obsessive
    compulsive, Out Of Order,
until he was himself ousted by Sam,
Sam who repeated the opening phrase (*"asherey ha'ish 'asher'*)
    of the Book of Psalms
as he handed Asher a Berbecker and Rowland
upholstery nail which Asher held as grim as grim
while sleeping on. Tonne upon tonne of clay, hay, hair, shoes
    and spectacle frames
made it less and less likely that we would land

on our feet on the Griggstown Causeway any time soon,
    Ramp Divides,
Please Examine Your Change As Mistakes Cannot Be
    Rectified,
the almost inaudible roar
of the millrace drowning out a great-grandfather's prayer.

By which authority did we deny Asher a mohel?
By which authority did we deny Asher a rebe?
Asher, meanwhile, slept on, his most crape-creepered of cribs
riding out the torrent, riding out the turmoil

of those thousands of Irish navvies piling clay, hay, hair into
    their creels
and bearing them at shoulder height, or above, with all the
    zeal
of creel catechumens. A tattoo on the left forearm
of some child-kin of my children, a very faint tattoo. Once
    more the storm
was howling and something, deh-dah, deh-dah,
something about that clay and hair going down the sluice
brought back an afternoon in St Louis.
Something about raking the ashes of the barbecue at the end
    of the verandah

and turning over the loin and flank
of a young peccary, its loin so lean and lank,
its little rib-cage, Road Narrows.
Something about turning over that runt of the peccary farrow,
with a dink and a dink
and a dinky-dick, brought back that afternoon. Something
    about Sam lighting a menorah
and reading a commentary on the Torah,
something about Arnie distancing himself from the 'night-
    and-fog' of Murder Inc.

to a disbelieving Duke of Wellington and Killadar of Perinda,
brought back the day
of our own *Nacht-und-Nebel Erlass*
on which I'd steadied myself under the Gateway Arch and
    pondered the loss
of our child. It was Arnie who'd been the brain behind
    running rum
to those thousands of Irish schlemiels
who dug the canal. A flicker from Asher's lids. The little
    whelks and wheals.
As if he might be dreaming of a Pina Colostrum

on Boscobel Beach, some young beauty dipping his foot in
    Johnson's baby oil.
Fanny peeked from her astrakhan, its poile
the poile of a stillborn lamb. Again a chainsaw letting rip.
Again I scrubbed the very latest in traps
while Helene rubbed cornstarch into whatever was curled,
    rawer and rawer,
in the autoclave. 'That peccary with the hind foot,'
the peaked cap would enquire, 'it's a bad case of *spina bifida*?'
I heard a bottom drawer

open somewhere. The red stain on the lint
that covered whatever it was in the autoclave brought back an
    afternoon in Poland
when the smoke would flail and fling itself, Maximum
    Headroom,
from a crematorium

at Auschwitz. It was not without some
trepidation, so, that I trained my camcorder
on this group of creel carters
bearing clay, hay, hair (at shoulder height, or above) through
  the awesome

morning after Hurricane Floyd as yet another 1921 Benz or
  1924 Bugatti
came down Canal Road and yet another peaked
cap was enquiring of my child-kin the meaning of '*Ashkenaz*',
Place Mask Over Mouth and Nose,
my trepidation becoming more and more
pronounced as that smoke would flail and fling itself over
  Auschwitz.
I looked up from our make-believe version of Boscobel Beach
to a cauterized stump of sassafras or sycamore

as the creel carters piled more and more clay, hay, hair,
  spectacle frames, *Willkommen*,
onto the line of carrioles and camions
by the edge of the flooded stream, those creel carters
  imagining in excited reverie
the arches of the bridge wrought with the motto *Albeit Macht
  Frei*,
while I looked up through the swing
and swale of smoke, Please Leave A Message After The Beep,
and watched the kebab-babby we had lost a year or two back
  put on its best bib
and tucker, watched it put out its little bit of a wing

all tinged with char
as if to set off for the real Boscobel Beach (on which we had
    met Sandra Hughes and Anton Hajjar),
oblivious to the piles of hair, spectacle frames, bootees and
    brogans
borne along from wherever. 'The full name is Auschwitz-
    Birkenau,'
Sam was explaining to Anton and Sandra,
who had somehow summoned themselves. Asher slept on, of
    course, despite his thrush,
despite his diaper rash,
the flood water having receded from the point on the driveway
    at which the pachysandra

had earlier been swamped, the point at which Arnie had fixed
    some class of a tow rope
to the chassis of the Studebaker. 'I simply don't have it in me to
    bribe
a ballplayer,' he would main-
tain, steadying himself with a handful of mane
as he hooked the rope to the hames of a draft mule, This Truck
Makes Wide Right Turns. The fact that the slew of interlocutors
in Asher's glabrous face now included, of all things, the peccary
    runt, Do Not Litter,
left me no less awestruck

than if the Studebaker were to be suddenly yanked back to the
    factory in South Bend
from which it had been packed off, Open This End,

than if the soul of one of the dozen stillborn
lambs sewn into Fanny's astrakhan were to recover radical
    innocence and learn,
than if scouring the trap by which I had taken that peccary, so
    lank and lean,
by its dinky hind leg,
Don't Walk, than if, Don't Walk, than if, Don't Walk,
than if scouring might make it clean.

An overwhelming sense of déjà vu. The creel caravan
swaying along the salt route into Timbuktu. Fanny taking up a
    hand-held microphone
and embarking on 'Secondhand Rose'. The convoy
of salt merchants setting down their loys
at one and the same moment. Our piliated woodpecker
    tapping at the bark
of three successive sycamores in the hope of finding one in
    tune.
The piles of clay, hay, hair, spectacle frames, hand-me-down
bootees and brogans now loaded onto the ark

causing it to lie so much lower in the water that Uncle Arnie
    gives a heavy hint
to Fanny that she should cut the chorus of 'Secondhand
Rose' and jump ship. 'The whitewall
tyre', Helene concurs, 'is the beginning of the pram in the
    hall.'
Asher sleeps on, attended by two teddy bears,
his soul less likely than ever to recover radical innocence and
    learn at last

that it is self-delighting. Ada Korelitz, Sam's widow, is
    drawing up A-, B-, and C-lists
of the Korelitz forebears

whom she'll invite to a reception thrown by herself and
    Arnie, Unapproved Road,
for the 1919 World Series-winning Cincinnati Reds.
'If there's no hatred in a mind,' Isaac Wolf
pounds and expounds, 'assault and battery of the wind can
    never tear the deh-dah from the leaf.'
'As for the killdeer,' Helene peeks from an astrakhan almost
    as natty
as Fanny's, 'you're thinking, in all likelihood,
of the killdeer of Perinda.' The ark now lies so much lower in
    the water, Stop Ahead,
that Uncle Arnie gives another heavy hint to the Cincinnati

Reds that they should also jump ship, *Achtung.*
The 1920 Studebaker's just one step ahead of a Panther tank
nodding approvingly through the ghetto after the Germans
    have massacred
the Jews of Bialystok. The wind bred on the Atlantic has
    broken Belmar and Seagirt.
Boundbrook is broken. The roof-levelling wind, profane and
    irreverent,
the wind which was at the spearhead
of the attack on the ark, almost inaudible. The memory of a
    three-month growth spurt
no more than a flicker, For Rent,

behind Asher's sleeping lids. The A-, B-, and C-lists of
  forebears in his glabrous face.
Hanff. Wolf. Reinhart. Abrams. A Reinhart beginning to fuss
as a peaked cap enquires about the Orthodox
position on the eating of white-lipped peccary. The train
  stopped in Bialystok's
running neither to Warsaw nor Leningrad.
Helene uttering a little cuss
as the yellow of that star brings back the out-and-out yellowness
  of a cylinder of gas
she once saw on Charing Cross Road. Now Isaac Wolf, a Yale
  grad,

looks on helplessly at the millrace on which sign-post, sign-
  board, Birdseed, Keep Out,
Bridge Freezes Before Road, Do Not Drive In Breakdown Lane,
  Live Bait,
my lonely helter-skelter, $500 Fine,
the makeshift oven
in which we meant, Keep Clear, All Directions, the Vermont
  decal
on that Bugatti-load of grain alcohol, Slow,
the out-and-out yellow
of the sign-post that points toward the place where the soul
  might recover radical

innocence, No Stopping Except For Repairs, the makeshift oven
  in which we meant to bake
the peccary *en croute*, Contents Under Pressure, the freezer bag

into which we've bundled the carry-out from the Sahara,
the sign-post that points to where the Missouri
had not as yet been swollen, Hump, No Shoulder, No Rail,
are all borne along, Toll Booth,
to where Uncle Arnie's father, Abraham Rothstein, one of the
    founders of Beth
Israel (yes, *Beth Israel*),

joins Fanny Brice in the version of 'My Man' she first sang in
    the Ziegfeld Follies.
A flicker from behind the lids. As if those children-kin might
    flee
as they fled the Cossacks in the Ukraine,
Please Remember To Take Your Belongings When You Leave
    The Train,
woken as they now are by a piliated Rowland and Berbecker
tapping into a sycamore. Asher's face a fox's mask
nailed to a long-gone door-post by an Irish schlemiel as likely
    as not to mosk
his brogans for a ladle of rum. 'What's with these police
    captains, like Charlie Becker,'

Arnie puts his arm around Helene, who, being chosen, finds
    life flat,
Contents May Have Shifted During Flight,
'who think they're above the law, who think they're born
    without belly buttons?'
The police launch manoeuvring by brings back riot shields
    and batons,

some child-kin of my children picking at his kohlrabi.
Now Helene leaves off rubbing cornstarch
into the arch
of whatever lies in the autoclave, sets the little beak of her
    Colibri

wobblingly to a cigarette, Pull To Open,
and reaches into a drawer for the poultry shears. The hacking
    through a babby bone.
No obstacle but Gregory's wood
and one bare hill, Slippery When Wet,
bringing back the morning Dr Patel had systematically drawn
the child from Jean's womb, For Hire,
Uncle Arnie all the while hanging a whitewall tyre
about the draft mule's neck, the draft mule no less thraward-
    thrawn

than whichever Waugh deemed the pram in the hallway the
    end of art.
The peaked cap sweet-talking that young Abrams or Reinhart
with the offer of a tin of waffeletten
should he feel able to enlighten
him on the particular house in the Bialystok ghetto
in which his uncle is hunkering down. Asher puts his lips to
    the shofar
of a long-gone pacifier
as Isaac Wolf expounds to Fanny Brice ('it's from *getto*, "a
    foundry", not *borghetto*,

a "borough"'), on that little gore, that little gusset
of ground into which my cast
of thousands of Irish schmucks have been herded, *Halt*.
Asher opens his eyes. Once more the storm is howling as it
    howled
when Isaac shouted down the board of Yale, the Black Horse
    Tavern still served ale,
when Sophie was found dead in the bath, a ringed plover
with all her rings stolen, Please Cover,
when Sam discontinued his line of Berbecker and Rowland
    upholstery nails, For Sale,

when we might yet have climbed the hill and escaped by
    Coppermine,
when Uncle Arnie was gut-shot (by George McManus?)
for non-payment of tight-lipped, poker-faced debts, when
    Helene Hanff, the celeb,
was found asleep
in the De Witt nursing home in the arms of Bulwer-Lytton,
    Follow Detour,
when Fanny tried to stop the leak
of a so-called confession by one Joseph Gluck
which fingered her ex-husband, Nicky Arnstein, when the
    trebucket of my lonely *túr*

was tripped for the very last time by Joe Hanff, No Egress,
    when a cantankerous
young Reinhart or Abrams, No Children Beyond This Point,
was borne along at shoulder height by the peaked cap, Out Of
    Bounds,

when the cry went up from a starving Irish schlemiel who
    washed an endosperm
of wheat, deh-dah, from a pile of horse-keek
held to the rain, one of those thousands of Irish schmucks
    who still loll, still loll and lollygag,
between the preposterous towpath and the preposterous berm.

from HORSE LATITUDES

At Least They Weren't Speaking French

At least they weren't speaking French
when my father sat with his brothers and sisters, two of each,
  on a ramshackle bench
at the end of a lane marked by two white stones
and made mouth music as they waited, chilled to the bone

fol-de-rol fol-de-rol fol-de-rol-di-do

for the bus meant to bring their parents back from town.
It came and went. Nothing. One sister was weighed down
by the youngest child. A grocery bag from a town more
  distant still, in troth.
What started as a cough

fol-de-rol fol-de-rol fol-de-rol-di-do

would briefly push him forward to some minor renown,
then shove him back, oddly summery, down
along the trench
to that far-flung realm where, at least, they weren't speaking
  French.

II

At least they weren't speaking French
when another brother, twenty-something, stepped on a nail
　no one had bothered to clench
in a plank thrown
halfheartedly from the known to the unknown

fol-de-rol fol-de-rol fol-de-rol-di-do

across a drainage ditch on a building site. His nut-brown arm.
　His leg nut-brown.
That nail sheathed in a fine down
would take no more than a week or ten days to burgeon from
　the froth
of that piddling little runoff

fol-de-rol fol-de-rol fol-de-rol-di-do

and make of him a green and burning tree. His septicaemia-
　crown.
Sowans as much as he could manage. Trying to keep that
　flummery down
as much as any of them could manage. However they might
　describe the stench,
as exhalation, as odour, at least they weren't speaking French.

III

At least they weren't speaking French
when those twenty-something council workers, one with a
    winch, the other a wrench,
would point my son and me to a long overgrown
lane marked by two faded stones

fol-de-rol fol-de-rol fol-de-rol-di-do

like two white-faced clowns
gaping at the generations who passed between them and set
    down
bag after grocery bag. Setting them on the table. The
    newspaper tablecloth.
1976. Not the East Tyrone Brigade, not Baader-Meinhof

fol-de-rol fol-de-rol fol-de-rol-di-do

bringing the suggestion of a frown
to those two mummer stones still trying to lie low, trying to
    keep their mummery down
to a bare minimum, two stones that, were they to speak,
    might blench
as much at their own giving out as our taking in that at least
    they weren't speaking French.

The Old Country

Where every town was a tidy town
and every garden a hanging garden.
A half could be had for half a crown.
Every major artery would harden

since every meal was a square meal.
Every clothesline showed a line of undies
yet no house was in dishabille.
Every Sunday took a month of Sundays

till everyone got it off by heart
every start was a bad start
since all conclusions were foregone.

Every wood had its twist of woodbine.
Every cliff its herd of fatalistic swine.
Every runnel was a Rubicon.

II

Every runnel was a Rubicon
and every annual a hardy annual
applying itself like linen to a lawn.
Every glove compartment held a manual

and a map of the roads, major and minor.
Every major road had major roadworks.
Every wishy-washy water diviner
had stood like a bulwark

154

against something worth standing against.
The smell of incense left us incensed
at the firing of the fort.

Every heron was a presager
of some disaster after which, we'd wager,
every resort was a last resort.

 III

Every resort was a last resort
with a harbour that harboured an old grudge.
Every sale was a selling short.
There were those who simply wouldn't budge

from the *Dandy* to the *Rover.*
That shouting was the shouting
but for which it was all over –
the weekend, I mean, we set off on an outing

with the weekday train timetable.
Every tower was a tower of Babel
that graced each corner of a bawn

where every lookout was a poor lookout.
Every rill had its unflashy trout.
Every runnel was a Rubicon.

IV

Every runnel was a Rubicon
where every ditch was a last ditch.
Every man was 'a grand wee mon'
whose every pitch was another sales pitch

now every boat was a burned boat.
Every cap was a cap in hand.
Every coat a trailed coat.
Every band was a gallant band

across the broken bridge
and broken ridge after broken ridge
where you couldn't beat a stick with a big stick.

Every straight road was a straight up speed trap.
Every decision was a snap.
Every cut was a cut to the quick.

V

Every cut was a cut to the quick
when the weasel's twist met the weasel's tooth
and Christ was somewhat impolitic
in branding as 'weasels fighting in a hole', forsooth,

the petrol smugglers back on the old sod
when a vendor of red diesel
for whom every rod was a green rod
reminded one and all that the weasel

was nowhere to be found in that same quarter.
No mere mortar could withstand a ten-inch mortar.
Every hope was a forlorn hope.

So it was that the defenders
were taken in by their own blood splendour.
Every slope was a slippery slope.

VI

Every slope was a slippery slope
where every shave was a very close shave
and money was money for old rope
where every grave was a watery grave

now every boat was, again, a burned boat.
Every dime-a-dozen rat a dime-a-dozen drowned rat
except for the whitrack, or stoat,
which the very Norsemen had down pat

as a weasel-word
though we know their speech was rather slurred.
Every time was time in the nick

just as every nick was a nick in time.
Every unsheathed sword was somehow sheathed in rime.
Every cut was a cut to the quick.

VII

Every cut was a cut to the quick
what with every feather a feather to ruffle.
Every whitrack was a whitterick.
Everyone was in a right kerfuffle

when from his hob some hobbledehoy
would venture the whitterick was a curlew.
Every wall was a wall of Troy
and every hunt a hunt in the purlieu

of a demesne so out of bounds
every hound might have been a hellhound.
At every lane end stood a milk churn

whose every dent was a sign of indenture
to some pig wormer or cattle drencher.
Every point was a point of no return.

VIII

Every point was a point of no return
for those who had signed the Covenant in blood.
Every fern was a maidenhair fern
that gave every eye an eyeful of mud

ere it was plucked out and cast into the flame.
Every rowan was a mountain ash.
Every swath-swathed mower made of his graft a game
and the hay sash

went to the kemper best fit to kemp.
Every secretary was a temp
who could shift shape

like the river goddesses Banna and Boann.
Every two-a-penny maze was, at its heart, Minoan.
Every escape was a narrow escape.

IX

Every escape was a narrow escape
where every stroke was a broad stroke
of an axe on a pig nape.
Every pig was a pig in a poke

though it scooted once through the Diamond
so unfalt – so unfalteringly.
The threshold of pain was outlimened
by the bar raised at high tea

now every scone was a drop scone.
Every ass had an ass's jawbone
that might itself drop from grin to girn.

Every malt was a single malt.
Every pillar was a pillar of salt.
Every point was a point of no return.

X

Every point was a point of no return
where to make a mark was to overstep the mark.
Every brae had its own braw burn.
Every meadow had its meadowlark

that stood in for the laverock.
Those Norse had tried fjord after fjord
to find a tight wee place to dock.
When he made a scourge of small whin cords,

Christ drove out the moneylenders
and all the other bitter-enders
when the thing to have done was take up the slack.

Whin was to furze as furze was to gorse.
Every hobbledehoy had his hobbledyhobbyhorse.
Every track was an inside track.

XI

Every track was an inside track
where every horse had the horse sense
to know it was only a glorified hack.
Every graineen of gratitude was immense

and every platitude a familiar platitude.
Every kemple of hay was a kemple tossed in the air
by a haymaker in a hay feud.
Every chair at the barn dance a musical chair

given how every paltry poltroon
and his paltry dog could carry a tune
yet no one would carry the can

any more than Samson would carry the temple.
Every spinal column was a collapsing stemple.
Every flash was a flash in the pan.

XII

Every flash was a flash in the pan
and every border a herbaceous border
unless it happened to be *an*
herbaceous border as observed by the *Recorder*

or recorded by the *Observer.*
Every widdie stemmed from a willow bole.
Every fervour was a religious fervour
by which we'd fly the godforsaken hole

into which we'd been flung by it.
Every pit was a bottomless pit
out of which every pig needed a piggyback.

Every cow had subsided in its subsidy.
Biddy winked at Paddy and Paddy winked at Biddy.
Every track was an inside track.

XIII

Every track was an inside track
and every job an inside job.
Every whitterick had been a whitrack
until, from his hobbledehob,

that hobbledehobbledehoy
had insisted the whitterick was a curlew.
But every boy was still 'one of the boys'
and every girl 'ye girl ye'

for whom every dance was a last dance
and every chance a last chance
and every letdown a terrible letdown

from the days when every list was a laundry list
in that old country where, we reminisced,
every town was a tidy town.

It Is What It Is

It is what it is, the popping underfoot of the bubble wrap
in which Asher's new toy came,
popping like bladder wrack on the foreshore
of a country toward which I've been rowing
for fifty years, my peeping from behind a tamarind
at the peeping ox and ass, the flyer for a pantomime,
the inlaid cigarette box, the shamrock-painted jug,
the New Testament bound in red leather
lying open, Lordie, on her lap
while I mull over the rules of this imperspicuous game
that seems to be missing one piece, if not more.
Her voice at the gridiron coming and going
as if snatched by a sea wind.
My mother. Shipping out for good. For good this time.
The game. The plaything spread on the rug.
The fifty years I've spent trying to put it together.

Turkey Buzzards

They've been so long above it all,
    those two petals
so steeped in style they seem to stall
    in the kettle

simmering over the town dump
    or, better still,
the neon-flashed, X-rated rump
    of fresh roadkill

courtesy of the interstate
    that Eisenhower
would overtake in the home straight
    by one horsepower,

the kettle where it all boils down
    to the thick scent
of death, a scent of such renown
    it's given vent

to the idea buzzards can spot
    a deer carcass
a mile away, smelling the rot
    as, once, Marcus

Aurelius wrinkled his nose
    at a gas leak
from the Great Sewer that ran through Rome
    to the Tiber

then went searching out, through the gloam,
    one subscriber
to the other view that the rose,
    full-blown, antique,

its no-frills ruff, the six-foot shrug
    of its swing-wings,
the theologian's and the thug's
    twin triumphings

in a buzzard's shaved head and snood,
    buzz-buzz-buzzy,
its logic in all likelihood
    somewhat fuzzy,

would ever come into focus,
    it ever deign
to dispense its hocus-pocus
    in that same vein

as runs along an inner thigh
    to where, too right,
the buzzard vouchsafes not to shy
    away from shite,

its mission not to give a miss
    to a bête noire,
all roly-poly, full of piss
    and vinegar,

trying rather to get to grips
        with the grommet
of the gut, setting its tinsnips
        to that grommet

in the spray-painted hind's hindgut
        and making a
sweeping, too right, a sweeping cut
        that's so blasé

it's hard to imagine, dear Sis,
        why others shrink
from this sight of a soul in bliss,
        so in the pink

from another month in the red
        of the shambles,
like a rose in over its head
        among brambles,

unflappable in its belief
        it's Ararat
on which the Ark would come to grief,
        abjuring that

Marcus Aurelius humbug
        about what springs
from earth succumbing to the tug
        at its heartstrings,

reported to live past fifty,
    as you yet may,
dear Sis, perhaps growing your hair
    in requital,

though briefly, of whatever tears
    at your vitals,
learning, perhaps, from the nifty,
    nay *thrifty*, way

these buzzards are given to stoop
    and take their ease
by letting their time-chastened poop
    fall to their knees

till they're almost as bright with lime
    as their night roost,
their poop containing an enzyme
    that's known to boost

their immune systems, should they prong
    themselves on small
bones in a cerebral cortex,
    at no small cost

to their well-being, sinking fast
    in a deer crypt,
buzzards getting the hang at last
    of being stripped

of their command of the vortex
    while having lost
their common touch, they've been so long
    above it all.

Medley for Morin Khur

I

The sound box is made of a horse's head.
The resonator is horse skin.
The strings and bow are of horsehair.

II

The morin khur is the thoroughbred
of Mongolian violins.
Its call is the call of the stallion to the mare.

III

A call which may no more be gainsaid
than that of jinn to jinn
through jasmine-weighted air.

IV

A call that may no more be gainsaid
than that of blood kin to kin
through a body-strewn central square.

V

A square in which they'll heap the horses' heads
by the heaps of horse skin
and the heaps of horsehair.

from MAGGOT

A Hare at Aldergrove

A hare standing up at last on his own two feet
in the blasted grass by the runway may trace his lineage to the
   great
assembly of hares that, in the face of what might well have
   looked like defeat,
would, in 1963 or so, migrate
here from the abandoned airfield at Nutt's Corner, not long
   after Marilyn Monroe
overflowed from her body stocking
in *Something's Got to Give*. These hares have themselves so
   long been given to row
against the flood that when a King
of the Hares has tried to ban bare knuckle fighting, so wont
are they to grumble and gripe
about what will be acceptable and what won't
they've barely noticed that the time is ripe
for them to shake off the din
of a pack of hounds that has caught their scent
and take in that enormity just as I've taken in
how my own DNA is 87% European and East Asian 13%.
So accustomed had they now grown
to a low-level human hum that, despite the almost weekly
   atrocity
in which they'd lost one of their own
to a wheeled blade, they followed the herd towards this eternal
   city
as if they'd had a collective change of heart.
My own heart swells now as I watch him nibble on a shoot
of blaeberry or heather while smoothing out a chart

by which he might divine if our Newark-bound 757 will one
   day overshoot
the runway about which there so often swirled
rumours of Messerschmitts.
Clapper-lugged, cleft-lipped, he looks for all the world
as if he might never again put up his mitts
despite the fact that he shares a Y chromosome
with Niall of the Nine Hostages,
never again allow his om
to widen and deepen by such easy stages,
never relaunch his campaign as melanoma has relaunched its
   campaign
in a friend I once dated,
her pain rising above the collective pain
with which we've been inundated
as this one or that has launched an attack
to the slogan of 'Brits Out' or 'Not an Inch'
or a dull ack-ack
starting up in the vicinity of Ballynahinch,
looking for all the world as if he might never again get into a
   fluster
over his own entrails,
never again meet lustre with lustre
in the eye of my dying friend, never establish what truly ails
another woman with a flesh wound
found limping where a hare has only just been shot, never
   again bewitch
the milk in the churn, never swoon as we swooned

when Marilyn's white halter-top dress blew up in *The Seven Year Itch,*
in a flap now only as to whether
we should continue to tough it out till
something better comes along or settle for this salad of blaeberry and heather
and a hint of common tormentil.

Lateral

In the province of Gallia Narbonensis and the region of Nemausus there is a marsh called Latera where dolphins and men co-operate to catch fish.
— PLINY THE ELDER, *Natural History*

In spite of a dolphin wearing through, every two hours, his
    outer layer
of conveyor-belt polymer, in spite of the spill of venom
by which his affiliates used to lure
mullet into their nets having taken its course
through his veins, he simply won't hear of how his affiliates
    outsource
their dirty work to another ring of the plenum.

Even the blue heron may backpedal
as he pins a medal
to his uniformed chest while vaunting cutoff denims,
yet a dolphin won't rethink his having left it to men
to send mixed signals to the mullahs they processed in some
    holding pen.

Quail

Forty years in the wilderness
of Antrim and Fermanagh
where the rime would deliquesce
like tamarisk-borne manna

and the small-shot of hail
was de-somethinged. Defrosted.
This is to say nothing of the flocks of quail
now completely exhausted

from having so long entertained an
inordinately soft spot for the hard man
like Redmond O'Hanlon or Roaring Hanna

who delivers himself up only under duress
after forty years in the wilderness
of Antrim and Fermanagh.

The Humours of Hakone

A corduroy road over a quag had kept me on the straight and
  narrow.
Now something was raising a stink.
A poem decomposing around what looked like an arrow.
Her stomach contents ink.

Too late to cast about for clues
either at the *purikura*, or 'sticker-photo booth', or back at the
  Pagoda.
Too late to establish by autolysis, not to speak of heat loss,
the precise time of death on the road to Edo.

Who knew 'forensic' derived from forum,
which senator's sword sealed the deal?
All I had to go on was this clog she'd taken as her platform,
this straight and narrow hair, this panty-hose heel.

I thought of how I'd once been inclined to grub
through the acidic soil
for a panty-hose toe or some such scrap
of evidence. Whereas Mount Fuji had yet to come to a head
  like a boil

about to crown its career,
it was too late to extrapolate from the cooling rate of fat
in a mortuary drawer
the rate of cooling in a body that threw off merely this sticker
  photo.

II

It was now far too late to know if this was even the scene of
   the crime.
Too late to ascertain from the serial number of a breast implant
if this was the same girl I'd seen in the *purikura* near the
   tearoom
back in Kyoto. Too late to determine if a salivary gland

might have secreted its critical enzyme
or, as her belly resumed its verdure,
implored an eye to give up its vitreous potassium
as a nun from a mendicant order

might unthinkingly draw in her voluminous
yellow robe to implore one for a little buckwheat.
Too late to put one's head into the noose
of the world as into the air pocket

of a capsized boat and swab the vitreous humour
off an eyeball. I'd read somewhere that the Japanese love of
   kitsch
is nowhere more
evident than in the craze for these sticker-photo booths which

go even further to reinforce
not only the heels of panty hose worn under a kimono
but the impression that phosphorus
might still be a common element in flash photography. Dead
   common.

III

Too late to determine how long the girl I'd also glimpsed at
the hot spring
had been beleaguered by pupae.
By day four the skin would have peeled from her thigh like a
fine-mesh stocking.
I thought of *De Mundi Transitu*. Columbanus at Bobbio.

I thought of how I'd planned not to keep my end of the
bargain
I drew up over that little cup of char
back in the Kyoka Ryokan.
I'd promised then I would willingly abjure

my right to eat globefish later that night in Santora
and enjoy my own little brush
with death. Too late to determine in which mountain sanitaria
the lepers had in fact been held. Too late to ascertain if Roshi

belonged to the Tokugawa clan with their triple-hollyhock mon
and their boat laid up for winter in shrink-wrap.
Who knew that *humus* might lie beneath 'humane'?
Too late to deduce if the father of this girl in her geisha robe

had met her mother on the main drag
of Waxahachie, Texas, while he worked on the
Superconducting Super Collider.
Too late to scour the scene for a kimono swatch or a toe rag
to send back to the lab for a culture.

IV

It was far too late to have forsworn
my ambition to eat globefish in an attempt to buck this
   tiresome trend
towards peace and calm. Too late to establish if the shorn
head of a mendicant nun might send

a signal back to the father of the girl I glimpsed on the
   Tokaido line
who had himself worked on the antilock
braking system of the bullet train. Too late to find a chalk
   outline
never mind the metallic

smell of blood on the corduroy
road to Edo. Too late for this girl to release an endorphin
to allow her to brave the *nishikigoi*,
or 'braided carp', which might have been the only ones to
   raven

on her foot soles. At Ryoan-ji a monk must rake and re-rake
the gravel with a birch-wood tine
till it looks like a series of waves always just about to break.
Too late to examine the small intestine

never mind swab vitreous potassium off an eyeball.
Too late to take in firsthand
the impression left on a sticker-photo-booth wall
of that great world at which this one may merely hint. Merely
   hint.

V

Too late to luxuriate in an *onsen*, or 'communal bath made of
   cypress',
and ponder an Elastoplast
that must have covered some minor bruise
winking from the depths. Too late to send it back to the analyst

with a swatch of sackcloth
or a panty-hose shred or a straight hair from her braid.
Too late to don a latex glove
and examine the corduroy road with its maggot brood

that traces itself back to the days of the Tokugawa shogunate
when Mount Fuji itself was coming to a head.
Who knew the body is a footnote
to the loss of its own heat

and the gases released when it begins to disintegrate
underlie a protruding tongue?
Too late to retrieve from the *onsen* in the shape of a giant gourd
that smelled like a lab's formaldehyde tank

her fancy-freighted skull that scarcely made a dent
in the pillow from which only buckwheat would now ever
   sprout.
Too late to divine from her stomach contents
the components of a metaphor that must now forever remain
   quite separate.

VI

It was far too late to reconstruct the train station bento box
she bought at Kyoto-eki the night before the night she took
  her vows
and threw up in the hollyhocks.
Too late to figure out if the Tokugawa clan would refuse

a plainclothes escort
to a less than fully fledged geisha.
Too late to insist that the body of a poem is no less sacred
than a temple with its banner gash

though both stink to high heaven.
Who knew that Budai is often confused with the Buddha?
Too late to divine
that what was now merely the air pocket of a capsized boat

had been a poem decomposing around a quill.
Too late to chart the flow
of purge fluid from a skull
that scarcely made a dent in the old buckwheat pillow

despite the metaphor that might have sustained her in her
  sorrow
as she, too, attempted to buck
this tiresome trend and alighted at the new station at
  Kazamatsuri
and felt, for the first time in years, the wind at her back.

VII

Whereas one might still try to reconcile the incorporeal
poem to the image of a fleshed-out Columbanus in a
  communal bath
his *Regula Monachorum,* or 'Monastic Rule',
hardly extended to the girl in the sticker-photo booth

who was yet to board the bullet train.
It was far too late to establish the interval
between her being so blissfully carefree and so balefully
  carrion.
Too late to deduce from the life cycle of a blowfly

a scenario that would not beggar
description less belief. Whereas I recognized the steel blue of
  one *Musca*
vomitoria, I couldn't connect the girl from the *purikura*
with the steel-blue mask

her sticker photo showed the world. The blowflies so few and
  far between
their threat must have seemed thinly veiled
until it was far too late to separate kimono and patten
from the black-green purge fluid.

Too late for the Tokugawa clan to send a galloper
over the bony ridge
in her skull with his accurate-to-within-a-thousandth-of-an-
  inch calipers
to report back to Edo on this security breach.

VIII

It was far too late to determine if these humours had been dry
   or wet
now I'd forsworn laying myself open
to the globefish. Too late to dissuade
the girl in the *purikura* from risking the type of panty-hose
   heel known as 'Cuban'

never mind warning her off a Hi-Chew flavoured with durian.
Far too late to inquire
why a poem had taken a wrong turn
on a corduroy road across a quaking mire

to have its own little meltdown.
I'd read somewhere that however advanced the art
of forensics has become, including the potassium analysis of
   the gelatin
in the vitreous humour, to fix the time of death is hard

if not hopeless. *Waxahachie.* Some propose the name means
   'fat wildcat'
while others persevere
in thinking 'buffalo creek' or even 'buffalo chips' just as good.
All I had to go on was the pouring of sulphur

over a clog print in snow, which seemed to highlight
that the poem began to self-digest
about the time I recognized that the sanitaria in which the
   lepers had been held
were nowhere in that great world of which this one is a
   sulphur cast.

IX

All I had to go on was the hunch that pupae would assail
the girl from the sticker-photo booth at the same rate as a poem
cadaver.
Who knew that *lepis* meant 'fish scale'?
All I had to go on was that a globefish would have gained its
livor

once it, too, was kitted out for the slab.
Whereas I'd read somewhere that the mean
annual temperature on Mount Fuji's slopes
was −7 degrees centigrade, it was nonetheless too late to
determine

if the humours of Hakone had been wet or dry.
Sanguine or phlegmatic. Choleric or melancholic.
In a drawer at the mortuary
a quail egg

from her railway-station bento
suggests the rate of cooling will vary by only a few degrees.
I'd read somewhere that the need for ID at the checkpoint
in Hakone started the sticker-photo craze

as far back as the Edo period. Along with the Japanese straight
perm.
Who knew that geisha is often confused with *geiko*?
All I had to go on was a single maggot puparium
to help me substantiate the date of a corduroy road over a quag.

Loss of Separation: A Companion

In the province of Gallia Narbonensis and the region of Nemausus there
is a marsh called Latera where dolphins and men co-operate to catch fish.
— PLINY THE ELDER, *Natural History*

I used to think that *Mutual Aid*
had given rise to the first kibbutzim.
Now an economic blockade
seems merely a victimless crime.

I used to think I'd got it right
when I notched up a '59 Plymouth fin.
Now I fight only to fight
shy of the assembly line

where I'm waiting for some lover
to kick me out of bed
for having acted on a whim

after I've completely lost the thread
and find myself asking a river
to run that by me one more time.

from ONE THOUSAND THINGS WORTH KNOWING

Cuthbert and the Otters

In memory of Seamus Heaney

Notwithstanding the fact that one of them has gnawed a strip
  of flesh
from the shoulder of the salmon,
relieving it of a little darne,
the fish these six otters would fain
carry over the sandstone limen
and into Cuthbert's cell, a fish garlanded with bay leaves
and laid out on a linden flitch

like a hauberked warrior laid out on his shield,
may yet be thought of as whole.
An entire fish for an abbot's supper.
It's true they've yet to develop the turnip clamp
and the sword with a weighted pommel
but the Danes are already dyeing everything beige.
In anticipation, perhaps, of the carpet and mustard factories

built on ground first broken by the Brigantes.
The Benedictines still love a bit of banter
along with the Beatitudes. Blessed is the trundle bed,
it readies us for the tunnel
from Spital Tongues to the staithes. I'm at once full of dread
and in complete denial.
I cannot thole the thought of Seamus Heaney dead.

In the way that 9 and 3 are a perfect match
an Irish war band has 27 members.
In Barrow-in-Furness a shipyard man scans a wall for a
    striking wrench
as a child might mooch
for blackberries in a ditch. In times to come the hydrangea
will mark most edges of empire.
For the moment I'm hemmed in every bit as much

by sorrow as by the crush of cattle
along the back roads from Durham to Desertmartin.
Diseart meaning 'a hermitage'.
In Ballynahone Bog they're piling still more turf in a cart.
It seems one manifestation of the midge
may have no mouthparts.
Heartsore yet oddly heartened,

I've watched these six otters make their regal
progress across the threshold. I see how they might balk
at their burden. A striped sail
will often take years to make. They wear wolf or bear pelts,
the berserkers. Like the Oracle
at Delphi, whose three-legged stool
straddles a fiery trough

amid the still-fuming heaps of slag,
they're almost certainly on drugs. Perhaps a Viking sail
    handler,
himself threatened with being overwhelmed,
will have gone out on a limb and invented a wind tiller
by lashing a vane to the helm?
That a longship has been overturned on the moor
is as much as we may surmise

of a beehive cell thrown up along the Tyne.
The wax moth lives in a beehive proper. It can detect sound
frequencies up to 300 kHz. The horse in the stable
may be trained to follow a scent.
What looks like a growth of stubble
has to do with the chin drying out. I straighten my
black tie as the pallbearer

who almost certainly filched
that strip of skin draws level with me. Did I say 'calamine'?
I meant 'camomile'. For the tearoom nearest to Grizedale
    Tarn
it's best to follow the peat stain
of Grizedale Beck. A prototype of backgammon
was played by the Danes. Even Mozart would resort to a
    recitative
for moving things along. Halfway through what's dissolved
    into the village

of Bellaghy, this otter steps out from under the bier
and offers me his spot. It seems even an otter may subordinate
himself whilst being first in line to revolt.
He may be at once complete insider and odd man out.
Columbanus is said to have tamed a bear
and harnessed it to a plough. Bach. The sarabande.
Under the floor of Cuthbert's cell they've buried the skull of
    a colt

born with a curvature of the spine.
Even now we throw down a challenge like a keel
whilst refraining from eating peach pits for fear of cyanide.
Refrain as in *frenum*, 'a bridle'.
We notice how a hook on the hindwing of a moth
connects it to an eye on the forewing. A complex joint
if ever there was one. According to our tanners,

the preservation of hides involves throwing caution
to the wind. Their work permits
allowed Vikings to sack Armagh in 832. The orange
twine helps us keep things straight. I once sustained
    concussion,
having been hit by a boom in Greenwich,
and saw three interlocking red triangles on my beer mat.
The way to preserve a hide is not by working into it Irish
    moss or casein

but the very brains
of the very beast that was erstwhile so comfortable in its skin.
Irish monasticism may well derive from Egypt.
We don't discount the doings of the Desert Fox
any more than Lily Langtry's shenanigans with Prince
Louis of Battenberg. The 1920s vogue for sequins
began with Tutankhamen. Five wise virgins

are no more likely than five foolish
to trim a fish-oil lamp to illumine
the process of Benedictine nuns spinning and weaving yarns.
I don't suppose we'll ever get to grips with the bane
of so many scholars–the word *SINIMIAINIAIS*
inscribed on a Viking sword. As for actually learning to
   grieve,
it seems to be a nonstarter. The floor of Cuthbert's cell is flush

with the floor of Ballynahone Bog after the first autumn rains,
the gantries, the Woodbines, the drop scones,
the overflowing basin's chipped
enamel, the earth's old ointment box, the collop of lox,
the drumroll of wrens
at which we still tend to look askance.
This style of nasal helmet was developed by the Phrygians

while they were stationed at Castledawson.
The barrow at Belas Knap was built before the pyramids.
Same thing with Newgrange.
The original seven-branched menorah's based on a design
by Moses himself. When it comes to the crunch
we can always fall back on potassium bromide
as an anticonvulsant. A camomile tisane

in a tearoom near the Bigrigg iron mine.
Since the best swords are still made from imported steel,
the more literal among us can't abide
the thought an island may be tidal.
This is the same Cuthbert whose chalice cloth
will be carried into battle on the point
of a spear. I can just about visualize a banner

of half-digested fish fluttering through the air
from the otter spraint
piled high at the threshold of Cuthbert's dry stone holt.
A sea trout is, after all, merely a brown trout
with wanderlust. It wears a tonsure from ear to ear
like any Irish aspirant.
We'll still use the term 'smolt'

of a salmon that first leaves fresh water for salt. Vikings will
    fletch
their arrows with goose long into the era of Suleiman
the Magnificent. A tithe barn
often cedes another tenth of its grain.
We won't have been the first to examine
our consciences at Bishop's Cleeve.
Benedictine monks will extend their tradition of persiflage

far beyond the confines
of Northumbria. Long after the Synod
of Whitby has determined the penis bone of an otter may
    double
as a tiepin. A grave's best filled with Lough Neagh sand.
We use a guideline when we dibble
cauliflower plants so things won't go awry.
A calcium carbide 'gun' still does duty as a pigeon-scarer

in the parish of Banagher, a parish where a stag
has been known to carry in its antlers
a missal, a missal from which a saint might pronounce.
Let's not confuse candelabras with chandeliers.
I'd as lief an ounce
of prevention as a pound of cure,
particularly when it comes to the demise

of a great skald. Coffin is to truckle
as salmon is to catafalque.
Could it be that both the trousers *and* the coat of mail
were invented by the Celts?
It's no time since Antrim and Argyll
were under Áedán mac Gabráin's rule.
We come together again in the hope of staving off

our pangs of grief. An altar cloth carried into battle
by the 82nd Airborne. A carton
of Lucky Strikes clutched by a GI on the bridge
at Toome. I want to step in to play my part
while the sky above the hermitage
does a flip chart.
Grey, blue, grey, blue, grey. However spartan

his beehive hut, Cuthbert has developed a niche
market in fur, honey, amber,
and the sweet wine we'll come to know as Rhenish.
Sometimes it takes only a nudge
to start a longship down a trench.
In 832, by most tallies, the Vikings did a number
on Armagh not once but thrice. I want that coffin to cut a
  notch

in my clavicle. Be they 'lace curtain' or 'shanty',
Irish Americans still hold a dirge chanter
in the highest esteem. That, and to stand in an otter's stead.
The chiastic structure of the book of Daniel
mimics a double axe-head.
As with the stubble, so with the finger- and toenails.
I cannot thole the thought of Seamus Heaney dead.

In South Derry as in the coalfields of South Shields
a salmon has been known to dance along a chariot pole.
In the way we swap 'scuttle' for 'scupper'
we're flummoxed as much by the insidiousness of firedamp
as our sneaking regard for Rommel.
I think of an otter cortege
passing under a colonnade of fig trees

barren despite their show of foliage.
We know neither the day nor the hour of our summons.
The same Cuthbert of Lindisfarne
whose body will be carried aloft by monks fleeing those same
    Danes.
Mountbatten of Burma. Montgomery of Alamein.
All with the same insignia on their scale-armoured sleeves.
Refulgent all. From *fulgere*, 'to flash'.

Pelt

Now rain rattled
the roof of my car
like holy water
on a coffin lid,
holy water and mud
landing with a thud

though as I listened
the uproar
faded to the stoniest
of silences . . . They piled
it on all day
till I gave way

to a contentment
I'd not felt in years,
not since that winter
I'd worn the world
against my skin,
worn it fur side in.

Saffron

Sometimes I'd happen on Alexander and Cleopatra
and several of their collaborators
tucking into a paella
tinged with saffron, saffron thought to be a cure
for scabies, bloody scours,
fires in the belly,

skin cancer, the ancient pestilence of Sumer,
not to speak of Alzheimer's
and plain old melancholy.
I'm pretty sure things first
started to look bleak in 1987 at the University
of East Anglia

where I was introduced to the art of the lament
by Ezekiel. His electric fire's single element
was an orange ice lolly.
He made me think I might lose my spot
as number one hod carrier in Mesopotamia,
a role that came quite easily

now I lived in a ziggurat
overlooking a man-made lake and sipped sugared
water with a swarm of honeybees.
Though A Flock of Seagulls
were scheduled to play the Union, there had been an icicle
in my heart since Anubis,

half-man, half-jackal,
had palmed me off on Ezekiel
for ritual embalmment.
He claimed A Flock of Seagulls were a one-hit wonder,
desert flowers left high and dry
on the polder. Anubis refused to implement

the Anglo-Irish Agreement.
He also told me the church clock in Crimond
had sixty-one minutes
to the hour. Ezekiel, meanwhile, was convinced
that creative writing, still in its infancy,
would amount

to a bona fide
academic pursuit only if students weren't spoon-fed
but came to think of literature
as magical rather than magisterial.
Saffron itself was derived from the three stigma-tufts of a
     sterile
crocus that, ground, were often adulterated

with turmeric. An icicle was formed
precisely because it would repeatedly warm
to the idea of camaraderie,
then repeatedly give in to chilliness.
I took comfort from the insistence of the anchoress, Julian,
on the utter

necessity of sin for self-knowledge, a theory I'd have to tout
to the Hare Krishna devotees
who'd sworn off sex outside procreation in marriage.
Sometimes I'd see one, late at night, in saffron robe and topknot,
stranded at a bus stop
on the outskirts of Norwich.

Cuba (2)

I'm hanging with my daughter in downtown Havana.
She's worried people think she's my mail-order bride.
It might be the *Anseo* tattooed on her ankle.
It might be the tie-in with that poem of mine.

The '59 Buicks. The '59 Chevys.
The '59 Studebakers with their whitewalled wheels.
The rain-bleached streets have been put through a mangle.
The sugar mills, too, are feeling the squeeze.

We touch on how Ireland will be inundated
long before the nil-nil draw.
Che Guevara's father was one of the Galway Lynches.
Now a genetically engineered catfish can crawl

on its belly like an old-school guerrilla.
Maybe a diminished seventh isn't the note
a half-decent revolution should end on?
The poor with their hands out for 'pencils' and 'soap'?

Hopped up though I am on caffeine
I've suffered all my life from post-traumatic fatigue.
Even a world-class sleeper like Rip Van Winkle
was out of it for only twenty years.

A fillet of the fenny
cobra may yet fold into a blood-pressure drug.
A passion for marijuana
may yet be nipped in the bud.

Some are here for a nose job. Some a torn meniscus.
The profits from health tourism have been salted away.
The blue scorpion takes the sting from one cancer.
Ovarian may yet leave us unfazed.

Hemingway's sun hat is woven from raffia.
He's tried everything to stop the rot.
He's cut everything back to the bare essentials.
His '55 Chrysler's in the shop.

We'll sit with Hemingway through yet another evening
of trying to stay off the rum.
I'm running down the list of my uncles.
It was Uncle Pat who was marked by a gun.

Our friends Meyer Lansky and the Jewish mafia
built the Riviera as a gambling club.
Had it not been for the time differential
Uncle Arnie might have taken a cut.

The best baseball bats are turned from hibiscus.
They're good against people who get in your way.
The best poems, meanwhile, give the answers
to questions only they have raised.

We touch on Bulat and Yevgeny,
two Russian friends who've since left town.
The Cuban ground iguana
is actually quite thin on the ground.

The cigars we lit up on Presidents' Avenue
have won gold medals in the cigar games.
Now it seems a cigar may twinkle
all the more as the light fails.

My daughter's led me through Hemingway's villa
to a desk round which dusk-drinkers crowd.
She insists the *Anseo* on her Achilles tendon
represents her being in the here and now.

The cattle egret is especially elated
that a plough may still be yoked to an ox.
Others sigh for the era of three-martini lunches
and the Martini–Henry single-shot.

When will we give Rothstein and Lansky and their heavies
the collective heave?
In Ireland we need to start now to untangle
the rhetoric of 2016.

The Riviera's pool is shaped like a coffin.
So much has been submerged here since the Bay of Pigs.
Maybe that's why the buildings are wrinkled?
Maybe that's why the cars have fins?

Dirty Data

The bog is fenced up there on Slieve Gullion, Slieve Gullion
   where the bracken leaf
still lies behind the Celto-Iberian sword design
adopted by the Romans. Pontius Pilate's poised with his
   handkerchief
at the parting spine

where the contestants snort and stamp.
That's right, Lew, the dealing
men from Crossmaglen put whiskey in our piñon tea. A
   hurricane lamp
shines from a shieling

like an undercover star. The goshawk nests in lodgepole and
   ponderosa pine
while a Mescalero girl twists
osiers into a basket that does indeed imitate

what passes for life, given how ring wants nothing more than
   to intertwine
with ring. The mountain's covered in heavy schists.
The streams themselves are muddied.

The dog is tense. The dog is tense the day Ben Hourihane
falls fuel of the new Roman turbine,
Little Miss Sally hisself, tense enough to set off a chain
of events that will see Ben mine

warehouse after warehouse of schlock
and link him via a Roman warship
to a hell-for-leather chariot race at Antioch.
Sooner or later Messala will need a lot more than a double hip

replacement while Ben will barely chafe
at the bit. That's right, Messala, an *amputation* saw!
The doctor is cocking an ear to your chest's tumble-de-drum

like a man trying to open a safe.
To add to the confusion, Ben's still trying to crack a lobster
    claw
with a lobster claw made of titanium.

Ben has somehow been playing scuffle on his washboard abs
while eating all that treif.
It looks like 1961. Or '65. No time before a few squatters from
the prefabs
in Dungannon morph into the crowd the paratroopers strafe

on Bloody Sunday. A golden dolphin marks the lap run by
each new
Roman tribune. Whitelaw. Pym. Rees. Mason.
Atkins. Prior. Hurd. King. Brooke. Mayhew.
Dense, too, the fog when each Halloween Ben ducks in an
enamel basin

for an enamel apple
and comes up with a botched job.
Such is the integrity of their kraal the horses will find no slot

in the funeral cortege of Winston Churchill from the Royal
Chapel
to Woodstock. As his carriage passes the dolphins bob
for a commoner's mere 19- rather than an all-stops-pulled
21-gun salute.

Along the Thames, meanwhile, even the cranes will bow
and scrape as the coffin passes the Isle of Dogs and the
    citizenry grapple
with their sense of loss. The *Havengore*'s prow
will no more shake off a water dapple

than we'll concede we've been excluded from a race.
It looks as if Little Miss Messala, played by a Belfast boy, will
    clutch
at the idea he might drive a tea-chest bass
to victory. Ben paces the afterdeck in the knowledge that as
    much

as we have sheltered them
our children will now feel obliged to shelter us
from some harshness we're not fit to bear. They'll glom onto
    the *gliomach*

shut out of its *lorica segmentata* while expecting us to
    condemn
wholesale the tattooed gulpin, the tatty glamour-puss,
not to speak of the other stuff they know we'll find hard to
    stomach.

That's right, Lew, you'll have Ben pace the afterdeck of a war
    galley
to which he's been consigned for having made an ad
    hominem
remark about a minister who banned a civil rights rally.
Though the top hem

of my childhood bedroom curtain's concealed by a pelmet
it clearly has the makings of a Roman cape.
Take the idea of a bird nesting in a bicycle helmet
some kid's hung by the garage door. The nest follows the nape

no less intently than the truth twisters and tub thumpers
will relocate your *Ben Hur: A Tale of the Christ*
from Judaea to an army outpost

near Jonesborough or Cullaville. These wouldn't be the first
    parachute jumpers
to have been enticed
into a honeypot and then by honeybees beset.

Sometimes the elephant in the room's the single war elephant
Caesar loosed on the Britons one bank-holiday weekend the
    traffic was bumper-
to-bumper. To add to the confusion, the evidence is scant
that the Hourihanes were ever actually reduced to eating
    Lumpers

in the 1830s. They may well have lived in the nether regions
of Tyrone where the Famine wouldn't hit so hard. That's
    right, Lew, they weren't swept
underfoot by the Ninth Legion
along with the rest of the evidence. Why did someone try to
    intercept

your letter to Billy the Kid? In 1933, Seosamh Mac Grianna
    would follow word for word
your purple-inked prose
as he rendered *Ben Hur* into Gaelic for An Gúm.

To add to the confusion the bird
has single-mindedly begun to transpose
materials from an abandoned site – cloak wool, horsehair, an
    eagle plume.

That's right, Lew, what we're looking at is a feather from a
    hawk or bald eagle
worn by the girl to whom you yourself transferred
your affections shortly after you were appointed to that regal
    (or *viceregal*)
post in New Mexico. Many of us remember how you'd gird

your loins for a three-day fact-finding mission
with Willie Whitelaw. That's when we first saw Messala
    twitch
through the partition
in a cowshed where he'd been tortured as a snitch

by four Mescaleros. Messala wouldn't have been the first
    soldier to marry
a local girl. Nor would he have been the first to spill
his guts under interrogation. Did Christ offer Ben water from
    an 1858 army canteen

or the 1874 model? It was on the rifle range at Barry's
amusement park that Ben may first have thought of
    countering the shoot-to-kill
policy by which Billy the Kid was gunned down.

Ben knows a Barrett semiautomatic rifle fitted with a Vari-X
    sight has got the job done
at distances of over a mile. There's really no way to parry
that infrared light. As to who masterminded the bomb run,
the records are almost as fragmentary

as the tile that clattered down from the roof of Ben's council
    flat
and spooked the prefect's mount.
The Lincoln County War, in which you tried to intervene,
    was another tit-for-tat
war fought between Prods and Papes. The body count

should include the glamour-puss Haya Harareet
as Esther. It must have been during the process of data capture
there was some mash-up of the 'coyote brush'

and her little 'pleat'.
Then there's Cathy O'Donnell, who plays Tirzah, 'she who
    brings rapture',
and on whom Messala might once have had a crush.

The shieling on Slieve Gullion. Oíche Shamhna. Messala's
    head shoved underwater
in a bucket. Hands tied behind him. A little meet and greet
with the Magna Mater.
Divination by fruit and nuts. As for the suggestion that the
    BNM stamped on those peat

briquettes stands not for Bord na Móna
but Banca Naţională a Moldovei, that's got to be a load of
    balderdash.
It comes as no surprise the Roman goddess Pomona
oversees a cache

of linen-factory data, albeit incomplete,
written on onionskin. It turns out that Ben Hur is a
    patronymic
meaning 'Son of White Linen'. 'Ben' like the 'Mac' in
    Seosamh Mac Grianna,

erstwhile political prisoner. A Loyalist gunman has been
    known to yell 'Trick or Treat'
as he opens fire with a semiautomatic. The dolphins continue
    to mimic
the obeisance of the dock cranes.

That's right, Lew, the obeisance of the dock cranes seems to
    mark another lap
of the Macedonian pirate fleet
around the Cinecittà tank. Why not fit a motion-sensitive
    booby trap
to the Canary Wharf bomb? A Pape had as much chance of
    winning a council seat

as a bird does of representing the abandoned site.
Yes, Lew, that Boston electoral district really did take the
    shape of a salamander.
The fact that Ben Hourihane's toga is lime-white
is emblematic of his essential candour

while the Barrett semiautomatic is seen to swivel
even as Little Miss Messala writhes
in anticipation of the amputation saw. As you drove out of
    Santa Fe in your gig,

Lew, it must have struck you that one way to cut through the
    drivel
is by welding scythes
onto the hubcaps of what was otherwise a regulation-black
    Humber Pig.

The pivotal point of Bloody Sunday sees a Humber Pig
   spinning its wheels
while Father Edward Daly has the Divil's
own job of escorting a dying man off the field. Many of us
   remember Whitelaw's spiel
about there being no granting of the privi-

lege of 'political status' to the prisoners in Magilligan and
   Long Kesh
despite the acknowledgement of their being 'special category'.
   It was by dint
of becoming tribune, Lew, you became enmeshed
in mortality. I think of George Bernard Shaw's household hint

about being patient with the poor funeral attendees who
   snivel
because they think they ought to live forever. Maybe it's best
   to put on our purple togs
and fall in with the cavalcade

that frolics and frivols
through the streets of Jerusalem to the Isle of Dogs.
The accoutrements of empire. The opportunistic bracken's
   rusting blade.

The loathsome Squirt Pig was so named because it was fitted
   with a water cannon
before which all resistance would be shown to shrivel.
It was deployed in Dungannon
in an attempt to cut down all that civil

rights stuff about 'One Man One Vote'. An extra in the
   parade was brought to book
for wearing a hackle on a Balmoral
instead of a tam-o'-shanter. Pomona wields a pruning hook.
In 1959, the same year *Ben Hur* took the laurels,

Seosamh Mac Grianna suffered the loss
of his wife and son. Both committing suicide. Both throwing
   off their yokes.
Mac Grianna would spend his final thirty-one years in a
   psychiatric

hospital in Letterkenny. That's right, Lew, each of us has his
   cross
to bear. An explosive charge fitted to the spokes
of one wheel will as readily put paid to the Ford Cortina as
   the Roman quadriga.

The cover of An Gúm's edition of *Ben Hur* sets it firmly in
   the Third Reich.
My childhood bedroom was divided by an earthwork fosse
that connected it to the Black Pig's Dyke.
The Squirt Pig, meanwhile, was painted in Admiralty-grey
   semigloss

meant to ward off those nightscopes. Disinformation about a
   dawn swoop,
half-truths and old-style spelling errors
only partly account for the imbroglio. Little Miss Messala and
   his skiffle group
doing their best to convince the reporter for the *Daily Mirror*

(as well as the stringers for Reuters
and Associated Press) they won't succumb to the Mop Tops.
   Now the surgeon cocks
an ear to Messala's chest and checks his pulse

though everywhere the world has missed the beat. That's why
   Lonnie Donegan loiters
with the intent of cracking the combination on the lock
and seeing everything fall into place.

'My aunt Jane, she's awful smart, she bakes wee rings in an
   apple tart.'
That's right, Little Miss, not only has Doctor Graves linked
   goitre
to a lack of iodine but he keeps on cocking his ear to the
   atrium of your heart.
The medical team is surveying you as a plough team might
   reconnoitre

a rolling mead. Try to hang in there. Don't forget how Jonah
was punished by God because he balked
at being a prophet. Some think the cult of that self-same
   Pomona
may be glimpsed in the apple tart. The Chiricahua leader,
   Victorio, has chalked

up so many defeats he's emerged the clear winner. The day
   you took the oath
of office was the day you found yourself trammelled.
The fiercely territorial 'Apache' goshawk is the same goshawk

(*an tseabhach mór*) that was sacred to Mars and Apollo both.
As for that most disinformative call about an 'apple' being
   made of 'enamel',
it's been traced to a South Armagh telephone kiosk.

That's right, Lew, when you installed yourself in the
    governors' palace
little did you think you yourself were part of the growth
and graft of empire. It's pretty clear Messala's guilty of malice
aforethought at Antioch just as it's pretty clear our children
    are still loath

to ascribe scythe-hubbed Ferraris to the Picts. Some see your
    failure to show at Shiloh
as the impulse behind *Ben Hur*. Pecs and abs, Lew, abs and
    pecs.
As for the idea that the bird casting its Lilo
upon the waters might be wearing an anachronistic Rolex,

that's not so much a blooper
as a timer for an improvised explosive device. The prow of
    the *Havengore*
continues to insinuate

itself into our consciousness. Billy the Kid lies in a stupor
while trying to grasp your offer of amnesty. Ben Hourihane is
    a lion chained to its roar.
Much as a disenfranchised Dungannon man is tied to his
    Nissen hut.

So it was that the funeral of Winston Churchill would
   gradually morph
into the funeral of an innocent victim of the paratroopers.
Father Daly. His handkerchief. The innocent victims of the
   bombing of Canary Wharf.
Two kinds of grass. Regular and super.

One need only tweak the Vari-X a smidgen
to make an adjustment
in windage or elevation. A canary is also a stool pigeon,
of course, someone who sings in an English accent,

the accent reserved for the Romans. The cars in the high-
   speed chase swap
insults as they cross the border. In the way Ben was asked to
   rat on his coreligionists
you asked Billy the Kid to turn informant. It's something like
   a badge

of honour that our children spare us the details of the
   undercover cop,
tattooed glipe that he is, tied by his ankles and wrists
and staked out over an anthill in South Armagh by the
   Chiricahua Apache.

'And when Halloween comes round, fornenst that tart I'm
   always found.'
The investigative team is pulling out all the stops
to establish if Mac Grianna's son committed suicide or
   drowned.
Because the bass player in the skiffle group has called so many
   Saturday-night hops

he manages surface tension with the grace of a common water
   strider.
It's easy to see how a UVF man posing as a B-Special
became a privileged insider.
Back in 1933, Mac Grianna had wondered if he should render
   'clockwise' as *deiseal,*

that being the direction in which a lobster (even one on a
   tether)
tended to move around a henge.
The British were still celebrating their victory over the
   Macedonian effetes

while every year at Navan Fort there was a hell-for-leather
chariot race in which redemption still somehow triumphed
   over revenge.
Now your bird is your wand, Lew. I'm fully aware of that.

I'm well aware that Ben Hourihane was sold cardboard shoes by
    a shoddy
millionaire from the North. Messala's hip was cobbled together
from a titanium ball-and-socket. With her bawdy
she thee warshipped, Lew, there in the nether

reaches of the *Havengore*. I'm also well aware that Judas Iscariot
doesn't play as big a role in the movie as in the book. As for the
    shtick
about the railway gauge being the width of a Roman chariot,
it was in Dungannon someone threw the half-brick

that set off the first of a line
of reinings-in of big parades. That's why it's pure chance the
    prefect would dodge
a paver or twice-baked *tegula* made of Coalisland clay.

That's right, Lew, pure chance the Mescalero girl to whom you'd
    taken a shine
would go on to dislodge
just such a tile from the roof of the governors' palace in Santa Fe.

It was in Barry's amusement park Ben had first found himself
    on a '3 Abreast Galloper'
and realized there was a fine line
between being bewildered and unfazed. That's right, Massa
    Lew, a caliper
isn't going to work. Lobsters really are a class of sea swine,

given how they grub
about in the shit. According to Sir Winston, such is the
    integrity of their limestone coral
the white-clawed crayfish love nothing better than to scrub
some data. No better place to start than with the Mescalero
    girl who refers to moral

turpitude as moral *turpentine.*
In your chest safe is the very handkerchief a nonplussed
Father Daly waved as a flag of truce on Bloody Sunday. When
    Pilate lets that hanky fall

it swerves as a morning to those who continue to wine and
    dine
on Massic and edible dormice, not to speak of the Seven
    Sleepers of Ephesus,
for whom this is indeed a wickiup call.

Index of Titles